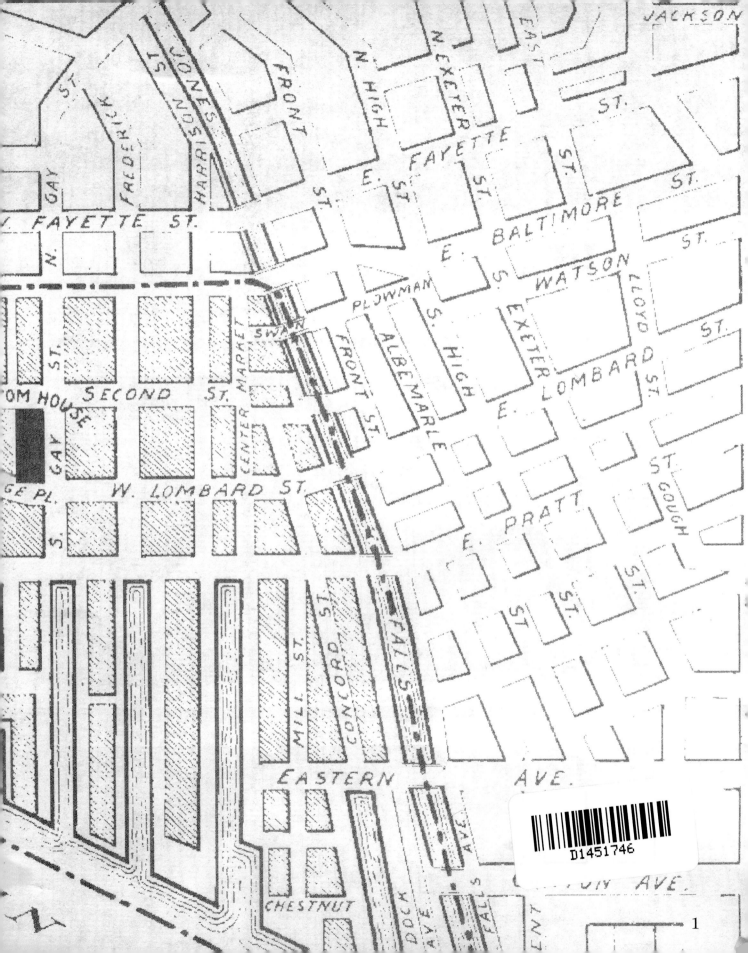

1

THE STORY OF THE GREAT BALTIMORE FIRE

by George R. Welden

Published in honor of his grandson, David Welden

2004
Fire Museum of Maryland
Lutherville, MD

ISBN: 1-891468-31-6

Printed in the United States of America
Editor: Melissa M. Heaver
Designer: Don A. Armbruster
Published by: The Creative Company Lawrenceburg, IN 47025, R. L. Ruehrwein, Publisher
Printed in the U.S.A. on recycled paper with vegetable inks. Text set in 12 point Caslon 224 Book
Cover Photo: Baltimore Street, c. 1:30 p.m., Sunday.
        Courtesy of Maryland Division, Enoch Pratt Free Library
End Papers: Welden adaptation of Sanborn Map of "Burnt District" – reproduced by the National
        Fire Protection Association.

Distributed by: Fire Museum of Maryland
1301 York Road
Lutherville, MD 21093
Phone: 410-321-7500
www.firemuseummd.org

CONTENTS

FOREWARD

George Russell Welden came by his love of the fire service naturally: his father, Walter Russell Welden, was a member of Engine Company No. 20 in the Baltimore City Fire Department. He had a knack for striping and lettering apparatus, so he was frequently assigned to the Repair Shop. George was a member of the Auxiliary B.C.F.D. during World War II but he couldn't fulfill his dream of going in full-time due to his poor eye sight. After the War he joined the Glyndon Volunteer Fire Co., Baltimore County and later was a founding member of the Chestnut Ridge V.F.C., where he served with distinction on the Building Committee and as the Training Officer.

In the 1960s Mr. Welden became a founding member of the local chapter of the Society for the Preservation and Appreciation of Antique Motor Fire Apparatus in America, and moved smoothly into the operation of the newly formed Fire Museum of Maryland in 1971. All this was natural for a man who lived for fire engines and fire fighting. I became acquainted with him during this period and I recall that he loved to regale his co-workers with stories of what it was like to live around the fire houses of yesteryear. Once he spoke of the new 'boiler engine' (the horse-drawn, steam pumping engine) being delivered from the factory; how magnificent it was in its gleaming, newly nickel-plated fixtures; and how the whole neighborhood turned out to admire its beauty.

Another time he spoke of how, as a child, he frequently played 'leap frog' over the cast iron hydrant covers: those two-foot high things that looked like mushrooms and protected the hydrant valve from the weather. George was always willing to share his knowledge of fire history, which was extensive, as he was a voracious reader. It was natural for him to study the events and effects of the Great Baltimore Fire of 1904.

By 1983 George Welden was ready to release his book 'No Reason to Burn!' having spent years researching how the Department actually responded to that monumental fire. He was the first to investigate the details of how each fire company responded during the first few hours of the Fire, and was able to conclusively show how the horse 'Goliath' factored into the saving of the 1898 Hale Water Tower. Unable to find a publisher, his book languished until Melissa Heaver, the Museum's Registrar, found an avenue to finally share this seminal work with the public. She began collecting photographic images to approximate as closely as possible, George's intentions. And she spent hours sympathetically editing and preparing the manuscript for the press. We owe a deep sense of gratitude to her for having undertaken this volunteer mission, in time for the One Hundredth Anniversary of the Great Baltimore Fire.

Finally, I would extend our heartfelt thanks to George's wife and life-long soul mate, B. Pauline Welden, for her gracious permission and enthusiastic support for this project. It is her wish that the book be dedicated to their grandson, David R. Welden, who continues the tradition of following the fire service lore. As his grandfather did before him, David today volunteers at the Fire Museum helping with exhibits and polishing brass on apparatus.

Stephen G. Heaver, Jr.
Director & Curator
Fire Museum of Maryland

ACKNOWLEDGEMENTS

Invaluable contributions to this story of the Fire were made by:

William A. Murray

Leslie E. Keller Sr.

Dr. William H. Engel, Jr.

Ruth Bowers

Ella Welden

Carl Tauber

Francis G. (Bud) McFarland

Loretta M. Burns

R. W. (Chie) Wigley

Willis Clayton Tull, Jr.

John Lewis

Keith Whitehurst

Andrew W. (Andy) Kohler

G.W. (1983)

The Fire Museum of Maryland would like to thank Mrs. Pauline Welden, wife of the author, for granting permission to the Museum to publish this book to commemorate the Centennial of the Great Baltimore Fire of 1904.

Additional contributions to the final compilation of this book were made by:

Debbie Brown

Curtis F. Elie

Gary E. Frederick

Stephen G. Heaver, Jr.

Jorene Kloch

Jeff Korman and his staff, Maryland Division, Enoch Pratt Free Library

Mark Mojdehi and his staff, Maryland Digital Cultural Heritage Project, Enoch Pratt Free Library

Denis Storck

MMH (2004)

To my father
Walter Russell Welden
Baltimore City Fire Department

G.W.

INTRODUCTION

This account of the Great Baltimore Fire of February 7-8, 1904 is a chronological story of the progress of the fire from the viewpoint of the firemen and from citizens who have shared with us their memories of that time.

Research has been based upon books, magazines, photographs, newspapers and personal stories, reinforced in the years following the fire by the author's intimate acquaintance with the geographic areas involved.

Every effort has been made to make this story of the fire as authentic as possible. Notwithstanding, reconstruction of events after three quarters of a century will contain errors or omissions.

If any reader has any information that will shed additional light on the subject, the writer would appreciate being informed.

George Welden (July 7, 1914 - August 22, 1989)

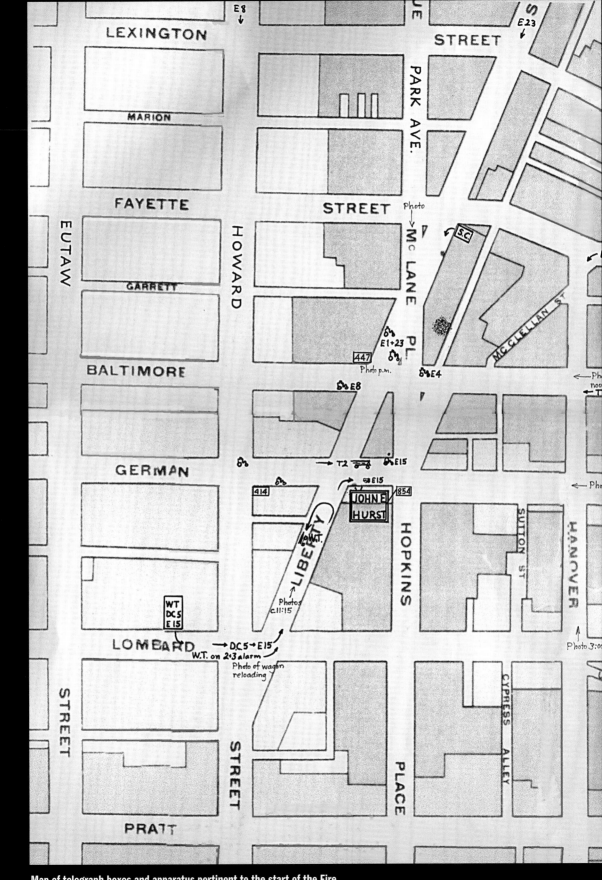

Map of telegraph boxes and apparatus pertinent to the start of the Fire.

THE BEGINNING

As the 20th century began, Baltimore was a thriving modern metropolis, clustered about the Patapsco River at the head of the Chesapeake Bay. The northwest branch of the river extended into the very heart of the city and was commonly known as "the basin". Here, bay steamers and sailing craft that served the many tributaries of the bay swarmed at the piers along Pratt and Light Streets. Larger ocean-going ships docked in the deeper waters of the outer basin around Canton Hollow and Locust Point, or in the middle branch to the southwest. The Jones

Within this area lay the commission houses, warehouses and wholesale houses, the financial institutional newspapers, hotels, retail districts and municipal and national government buildings.

Battle Monument at Calvert & Fayette Streets - before the Fire

Baltimore was known as the Monumental City by virtue of the magnificent shaft crowning the heights at Charles and Monument Streets, honoring the father of our country, George Washington; the Battle Monument, commemorating the deeds of her heroes of the

Photographer: Henry Rinn, Jr.

Baltimore Street, Looking West from bridge - before the Fire

Falls, a sizeable stream about 100 feet wide, flowed through the city between stone flood control walls, emptying into the eastern edge of the basin at City Dock.

From the waterfront the land rose gradually for approximately eight blocks to the north and the west, the last few blocks rising quite sharply to a high point near Charles and Lexington Streets.

Waterfront from Federal Hill - before the Fire   Photographer: Henry Rinn, Jr.

War of 1812, and other monuments throughout the city in testimony to her leading citizens. In the business district modern masonry buildings lined the streets on an average of four to five stories in height, with a goodly number of buildings of fire resistant construction ranging to heights of fourteen stories or more. Roofs were mainly of tin or slate, with some of gravel or shingle. The streets were paved with either cobble stones, brick, Belgian Block, or in some areas, wooden blocks. Basements of many buildings served as storage areas, extending out beneath the sidewalks. Glass disks, about two inches in diameter were set in the sidewalk to provide

"Dead Eyes" or vault lights: glass discs set in the sidewalk to provide light to the basement. It was through a broken disk that the kindling spark is believed to have entered. Photographer: Wayne Schaumberg

some light for the spaces below, and were commonly known as "deadeyes". In many places they were crazed, broken or missing completely.

All lines of power and communication were carried overhead. A forest of tall telephone poles, some at crazy angles, lined the streets. Many were taller than a five story building, supporting near their tops as many as 10 or more cross arms, like the branches of a tree. These cross arms carried a perfect maze of wires. Trolley-wires and their supporting cables covered the streets below.

Frameworks for awnings extended from building to curb.

Windows on the upper floors of even the tallest buildings were shaded by awnings. Signs and banners proclaiming the merchants' wares hung in profusion. The air space above the city streets was almost totally utilized. Fire Chief George W. Horton had complained that the wires split the hose streams and that the placement of ladders at fires was difficult due to these obstructions.

"Downtown" was the hub of activity. Streetcars, the prime mode of transportation, carried the people to work in the morning and took them home at night. Many workers walked to work, as a dense residential area ringed the business district.

For protection against fire, many of the commercial and industrial buildings in town were equipped with the Baltimore National Automatic Fire Alarm System.

Diagram of National Automatic Fire Alarm Co. Fire Alarm System. Such a system was installed in the John E. Hurst Building.

Howard & Lexington Streets: Prior to 1904, awning frameworks & wires took over airspace throughout the City. They caused problems during fires, as water bursts were split and had much less power.

Photographer Henry Rinn, Jr.

This system was comprised of a series of thermostats attached to the ceilings throughout the building on approximately ten foot centers. Each thermostat had two contacts, one contact set to indicate a temperature of 130° F heat, the other contact to indicate fire at 150° F. There was also an indicator to warn of an electrical fault in the system. All thermostats were connected to a numbered indicator box with a dial face on the outside of the building. An arrow on the dial would indicate the need for attention, or the floor location of high temperature or fire.

This system was connected to the Baltimore National Automatic office at 230 East Lexington St., the Baltimore City Fire Alarm Office in the City Hall, and the insurance companies sponsored Salvage Corps. All signals transmitted over the system were received at Baltimore National Automatic. If the flame sensor activated, the message automatically went to three services, Baltimore National Automatic, the Baltimore City Fire Department, and the Salvage Corps. On receiving the alarm, all companies assigned to that box number would respond. If the signal indicated a temperature rise, it would only register at Baltimore National Automatic. In this case, the Baltimore National operator would dispatch a messenger to the location to notify the occupants or watchman. If the building was closed, the messenger would then notify the nearest fire company. The fire company would then

dispatch a piece of equipment and make an investigation.

On the fateful Sunday morning of February 7, 1904, at 10:23 a.m. one round of box 854 registered at Baltimore National Automatic, indicating a rise in temperature. For one reason or another, it is rationalized the messenger was not available. Perhaps he was on another errand. Company procedure specified dispatch of a messenger, any other notification would be an infraction of the rigid rules. A phone call identifying the box number would be a dead give-away.

Engine 15 House, north side of Lombard Street, west of Howard Street. Home of Clapp & Jones Steam Pumper which was crushed by the falling walls of the Hurst building.

In any case, an anonymous telephone call was said to have been received at Number 15 Engine, requesting them to make an investigation at German and Liberty Streets, no building specified. A hose wagon and crew was dispatched to the intersection. On seeing no evidence of fire, they returned to their station without alighting from the wagon.

12

February 7, 1904 began as a raw, cloudy, blustery 40° day. Dirty patches of an earlier snow still lay in the streets. A twenty-mile-an-hour wind from the southwest was enough to cause flags to snap in the breeze and send bits of paper scurrying along the all but deserted streets. It was Sunday morning, and Baltimore was either in church or at home with the papers.

Number 15 Engine, Lombard Street near Howard was what was known as a double house. Stationed within were two engine companies, designated 15-1 and 15-2, each comprised of a steamer drawn by three horses and hose wagon, drawn by two horses. There was also a water tower drawn by three horses and the 5th District Chief Engineer's buggy. The horses stood in stalls along the walls of the house near their respective wagons. The men, in their dress uniforms, were getting ready to line up for the daily 11:00 inspection.

About the same time, David Rothschild, a Washington attorney, was making his way up Liberty Street, north of Lombard, with the wind biting at his back. As he approached German Street, he noticed smoke coming from the cellar of the building at German and Liberty Streets. Galvanized into action he ran to a nearby officer, Fire Patrolman Archibald McAllister, excitedly pointed and proclaimed "I believe that building is on fire!"

Turning, the officer agreed, and both headed for the nearest fire alarm box. As they ran, the gong in the Salvage Corps, two blocks away, could be heard. Rothschild's cry had drawn the attention of others. Mr. A. Summerfield, a wholesale clothing merchant from Durham, N. C., heard the cry and saw the smoke. John Conlon, a watchman in the National Exchange Bank, Liberty and German St., heard the cries of fire and went to a window on the German Street side of the building. Looking out, he saw flames coming from the top floor of the Hurst Building across the street. The John E. Hurst Company was a wholesale dry goods house. Their salesmen, or drummers as they were called, sold their wares to retailers throughout the south. Built in 1896, it fronted on Hopkins Place and extended along German Street to Liberty Street. Six stories high, it was built of brick with double boarded wood floors and joists resting on exposed steel beams. The beams were supported by cast iron columns. Near the center of the building, a fourteen foot square opening extended from the basement to the sixth floor. Within this opening were a passenger elevator and a stairway. Elsewhere in the building were two enclosed freight elevators. The building was fully stocked with merchandise for the coming spring trade. A highly combustible supply of celluloid notions, collars, combs, cuffs, some 100 dozen celluloid shirt bosoms and novelties filled the top floor.

As with most conflagrations, the exact nature of ignition may never be known. The Insurance Underwriters Committee reported in part as follows;

Hurst Building - before Fire

"At different times some of the 'deadeyes' had been broken in the sidewalk vault light and had been replaced. We assume that there was one or more broken at the time of the fire and that the high winds that prevailed on Saturday must have carried either a lighted cigarette, cigar or match through one of these holes into the basement. The stock directly under the vault lights consisted of blankets and cotton goods in cases, the covers being removed, and it is our opinion that the fire dropped into one or more of these cases, ——." As the building was closed at noon Saturday and unattended,

4th District Engineer John Kahl

the materials smoldered for some time, possibly overnight, generating smoke and gases through the flue of the open elevator shaft to the top floor, the smoke began to bank down floor for floor, until the upper floors became tightly charged with highly combustible gases. The whole building became a bomb, waiting to be triggered.

At 10:48 a.m., the alarm sounded on the gongs in the engine houses, '*automatic box 854, John E. Hurst Company, Liberty and German Streets*'. Responding from two blocks to the north the Salvage Corps was first on the scene. Captain Malcolm Jordan jumped from the wagon and ran to Baltimore and Liberty Street to pull Box 447 at 10:51 a.m., within three minutes of the automatic alarm.

At 15 Engine, Captain John Kahl had just completed inspection of the apparatus and the horses' harness when the gong struck. The chains on the stalls dropped and the horses

trotted into position under the suspended harness. Still in dress uniform, the men pulled the "spider" holding the harness down onto the horses' backs and snapped their collars in place. The "spiders" released and sprang back to the ceiling.

Steamer 15-1 and Hose Wagon 15-1 clattered out on to Lombard Street and swung left. Crossing Howard Street they turned left again into Liberty Street for a one block dash to German Street. Turning right on German Street, the hose wagon pulled up by the front door on the German Street side of the Hurst Building at about the same time as the Salvage Corps. Steamer 15-1, driven by E. Stewart, followed closely, turned left on Hopkins Place and took the plug on the northwest corner of Hopkins Place and German Street.

5th District Engineer Levin H. Burkhardt

Captain Kahl jumped from his seat on the hose wagon, ran to the box on the wall of the building and read the dial. The arrow indicated a fire in the basement. Meanwhile, Truck 2, a Hayes aerial ladder truck commanded by Captain Emil Heise pulled up and took position opposite the building on German Street.

Breaking open the door with a crow bar, Captain Kahl and his men entered with a chemical line, a rubber hose connected to a soda/acid tank on the hose wagon. Going to the open elevator shaft in the center of the building, they saw flame drawing across the ceiling to the shaft. Very little smoke was seen on the first floor or in the basement.

Descending the stairs to the basement, they found fire in open crates of blankets and dry goods, directly beneath the "deadeyes" in the sidewalk above. The flames and smoke immediately increased in intensity. Calling for the 2 1/2 inch line, captain and crew hastily withdrew from the basement, meeting 5th District Engineer Levin H. Burkhardt and the men of 2 Truck. Recognizing the situation, Burkhardt ran to German and Howard Streets and sounded the "four twos", a third alarm on Box 414, also calling Engine Companies 17 and 18. The time was now 10:55 a.m., just 7 minutes after the automatic alarm.

Meanwhile, inside the building, as the 2 1/2 inch line was being directed down the elevator shaft, Captain Kahl heard doors slamming on the floors above. His first thought was that a watchman was closing the doors. More likely it was the effect of the air entering through the open door reaching up the shaft. Suddenly there was a downward rush of dense black smoke down the shaft that filled the area, and all hands made for the door.

As they reached it there was a terrific explosion in the upper floors. The intense pressure within vented through all windows above the first floor, sending glass in all directions with a peculiar whistling sound. Captain Kahl, Harry C. Showacre, Guy S. Ellis and John D. Flynn were blown through the doorway and sent sprawling into German Street. Jacob Kirkwood, Jr. landed in a heap just inside. Regaining their feet, the men, with the aid of members of No. 2 Truck dashed back into the building and dragged Kirkwood out and across the street to safety amid a shower of debris.

David Rothschild, the attorney, was knocked flat to the sidewalk, got to his feet and took off. S. F. Ball, standing a block away on Baltimore Street, was cut on both hands and a hole was knocked in his hat. Harvey R. Baker, standing in a nearby alley, was stunned by the blast and walked almost a block in this condition before realizing his new $2.50 derby hat was on fire and cut by glass. John Conlon, the watchman in the bank, witnessed the explosion as the flames burst forth with a roar. The force of the blast opened a gaping hole in the west wall of the building near the roof. Although the walls did not rupture, the entire building immediately took fire, the force of the

Hale Water Tower. Firemen pose with Tower near Engine House #15 on Lombard Street. Young man on side step is messenger boy.

Horse "Goliath". Entered Fire Service on July 13, 1899 at age of six; retired after 19 years of service. Served as "off horse" on steamer, which meant he was placed on right side of the 3 horses that pulled steamer. He arrived nearest to the sidewalk and the Hurst Building when called to the Fire.

explosion driving the flames into and through the surrounding buildings.

Drawn by three horses, the water tower came dashing up Liberty Street in answer to the alarm. As it drew abreast of the Hurst Building, a tongue of flame lashed

Site of Thomas Burk's Saloon, also known as The Old Carpet Loom. Built 1745; stood on Southwest corner of German (now Redwood) and Liberty Streets.

University of Maryland Medical School to gather for the free lunch and soup prepared by Mrs. McFarland. It was among the first to take fire. West of the tavern, on German Street, the buildings faced north, presenting a solid brick wall to the fire. The space created by the low structure of the tavern and the brick side wall of the building to the west, together with the direction of the wind and the efforts of the firemen, prevented further extension of the fire to the west.

On the northwest corner, the wholesale drug house of Carr, Owens and Heineman, a four story brick building facing Liberty Street took fire. From here the flames swept

Carr, Owens & Heineman, wholesale drug house bottle

across Liberty Street to the National Exchange Bank.

It was from these windows that John A. Conlon had watched the drama unfold. At Maryland General Hospital, his face, head, hands and arms in bandages, he related what happened. Going to a window on the German Street side on hearing cries, he saw flames coming from the top floor of the Hurst Building. *"In an incredibly short time, the whole top of the building was in flames. Realizing that the fire might spread to our building, I at*

out, across the street, badly searing the off horse, "Goliath". In pain the beast shied away from the flame, causing the team and the water tower to reverse direction in Liberty Street and head south. They were brought up by the hostler just south of the Hurst Building, unhitched and led to safety.

On the southwest corner of German and Liberty Streets stood a three story and attic frame building, almost 160 years old, reputedly the oldest building in town. Originally the Old Carpet Loom, it had for years been occupied by Burk's Tavern. Just the year before, it had been purchased by James M. McFarland. McFarland had gone to work for the B&O Railroad at the age of 13 and had saved his earnings. Some twenty years later, in 1903, he left the railroad, married, and bought Burk's Tavern and its name. With the bar on the ground floor, a restaurant on the second, and barrels of whiskey stored on the third, it was a popular spot for students from the nearby *once got down the hose, which was in the building for use in case of fire. Before I was aware of it, the windows on the German Street side of the bank were afire. I began to fight the flames with the water in the building, but I was soon forced out of the banking room. I opened the door on the Hopkins Place side and asked a fireman to come in and help me. He refused. By this time the interior of the room was afire and I did not realize my perilous position until I felt a pain in my face. Then my clothing caught fire and I started to flee."* The intense heat had warped the iron doors, making him a prisoner. On being rescued he was taken to a hospital, severely burned about the face and body.

By now, fire companies responding to the alarm had several good hose streams going in German and Liberty Streets. One steamer was at work west of Liberty, and another was taking the plug and unhitching its team at Howard and German.

The sound of the explosion had shattered the Sunday quiet. Many, on their way to church, were drawn to the scene. Soon the streets were crowded with spectators, interfering with the apparatus and the efforts of the firemen.

About this time, Chief Engineer George W. Horton arrived on German Street, west of Liberty, in time to see Engine 15-1, its hose wagon, and Truck 2 burning furiously and out of reach due to the heat.

Chief Engineer George W. Horton

After directing placement of several lines of hose, Chief Horton hastened to make a survey of the situation. Looping North around the fire,

Hopkins Savings Bank

he passed south behind the Hopkins Place Savings Bank Building to German Street, east of the fire. After a careful survey, he decided to send to Washington, DC, for assistance. Being unable to go west because of the intense heat, he returned to Baltimore Street by way of Hanover Street. Meeting Police Lieutenant Charles M. Cole, he requested him to telegraph Washington for help. Running to the Secretary of the Board of Fire Commissioners Pinkney Whyte

Pinkney Whyte Wilkinson, Secretary-Board of Fire Commissioners

Wilkinson, Chief Horton ordered him to have the fire alarm office call all companies to the fire and place Reserve Engine 23 at the intersection of Baltimore and Charles Streets. "This is going to get worse", he said. "Tell them to send everything we've got! Everything!" Wilkinson ran to the Salvage Corps Station at Liberty and Fayette Streets, about a block away, and placed the call.

From a vantage point on German Street, J. E. Henry, a photographer, aimed his camera east to record the start of the conflagration. At 11:05 a.m., seventeen minutes after the automatic alarm, a tremendous explosion raised the roof of the Hurst Building and sent a billowing cloud of brownish smoke skyward to the north-east as part of the west wall of the build-ing disappeared.

11:05 a.m., Sunday Morning- Explosion in the Hurst Building, seventeen minutes after the automatic alarm sounded. View east on German (now Redwood) Street. Horse-drawn steamer at corner of Howard and German Streets.

Photographer: J.E. Henry

At 11:20 a.m., falling brick warned Captain Heise of Truck 2 and his men, who fled for their lives as the north and east walls of the Hurst Building came crashing down, burying Engine 15-1, its hose wagon, and Truck 2 beneath a pile of rubble. By 11:25 a.m., the building was down. Fortunately, by this time, police had the crowds in German Street safely behind lines west of Howard

11:20 a.m., Sunday Morning: Walls of the Hurst Building start coming down, burying Engine 15 and Truck 2 beneath rubble.

Photographer: J.E. Henry

Street. The fire then proceeded to burn the west side of Hopkins Place as well as the east side of Liberty Street from Baltimore to German Street.

Along Hopkins Place to the east, the buildings facing the Hurst Building, their walls parallel to the course of the fire, felt the full force of the blast. The flames entered through the window openings and extended through and out the rear. Then an iron box, containing about 60 lbs. of gun-powder, stored on the sidewalk in front of Findley, Roberts & Company

Photographer: J.E. Henry

11:27 a.m., Sunday Morning: Twenty minutes later, the Hurst Building is down. Horses detached and steamer at work with another steamer and aerial ladder in German Street. Crowds behind fire lines.

Hardware, northeast corner of Hopkins Place and German Street exploded. The blast threw men from their feet, shattered windows and doors in the entire neighborhood, and six more buildings in four different blocks were on fire before any apparatus could be brought into effective positions.

German Street, at this point, was a mere twenty feet wide. From here, the fire drove northeast through the middle of the block on Hopkins Place, through to the Roxbury Rye Company on the south side of Baltimore Street, midway between Hanover and Hopkins Place. Then the fire began to work its way back west to Hopkins Place. Next it jumped across Hopkins Place to the west side below

Baltimore Street. Shortly after noon the entire block bounded by Baltimore, Liberty, German Streets and Hopkins Place was a mass of flames. Before 1:00 o'clock, it was in ruins and burning furiously. On the northwest corner of Baltimore and Liberty Street, the four story Baltimore Bargain House burned.

Morton C. Stout Company, tailors, to the north on Liberty caught fire and burned. Two stores adjacent to the north caught fire but were saved, thus controlling extension of the fire to the northwest. Stored at A. Rupert's and Company, bookbinder, 135 South Sharp Street were a number of old and very rare volumes belonging to the Peabody Library. They were saved by Mr. Peabody at great personal risk. Daniel Miller, another dry goods house, adjoining the Hurst Building to the south was burned out from top to bottom by 1:00 o'clock.

The fire, having begun in the upper floors of the Hurst Building, and being blown into and through the upper floors of adjacent buildings by the force of the explosion, pursued this lateral course throughout the business district. The upper floors would be burning fiercely before hose streams could be brought into play. In this manner, it was unique, because in most conflagrations most buildings would burst into flame from radiant heat.

In an effort to contain the fire south of Baltimore Street, the chief ordered 4 Engine to the northeast corner of Baltimore and Liberty Streets, and directed Chief August Emrich to take a hose line into a building on the southwest corner. These orders he had to counter-

mand in minutes due to the rapid advance of the flames. The building on the northeast corner of Baltimore and Liberty then took fire in the mansard roof. Here he attempted to form a water curtain. Engines 1 and 23 were ordered into north Liberty Street. A line was taken to the roof of the adjoining Mullins Hotel a narrow, seven-story "L"

Deputy Chief Engineer August Emrich

shaped building fronting on Baltimore Street and extending around to Liberty. Within five minutes the entire building, as well as the buildings within its crook, was in flames. By 1:30 p.m., the fire was in possession of the northeast corner and Engine 4 was ordered out in the nick of time. The fire had jumped Baltimore Street. However, the companies in Liberty Street were successful in holding the east side, and stopping it just short of emergency headquarters in the Salvage Corps at Liberty and Fayette Streets.

Brands from the fire flew high overhead to

Front Street Theater   Photographer: Henry Rinn, Jr.

the northeast some eight blocks or more. The roof of the Zion Church School, Gay Street near Lexington, caught fire, causing the laymen to be dismissed. Carrying buckets of water to the roof, they extinguished the blaze. Farther east, across the Falls, the roof of the Front Street Theater also caught fire, damaging the southwest corner of the building. It was extinguished by the firemen.

Mayor Robert M. McLane and his staff, City Engineer Benjamin T. Fendall, Building Inspector Edward D. Preston and Joseph L. Wickes had toured the fire lines and were now trying to determine a course of action. Also present was ex-chief of the Fire Department William C. McAfee whose advice was solicited. It is claimed that the idea of using dynamite originated with Inspector Preston in a conversation with George May at Sharp and Lombard Streets

Mayor Robert M. McLane

Chief William C. McAfee

at about 1:00. Preston is then said to have conferred with Chief Emrich and District Engineer Burkhardt and they are said to have agreed. After a long discussion by the Mayor and his advisors, it was decided to dynamite.

Mayor McLane called his friend Patrick Flanigan, a contractor, and Roy Lafferty, a former army engineer, to do the job. The Flanigans, father and son, hurried to the Peddicord and Atchinson Quarries on Falls Road and loaded four or five wagons with several thousand pounds of dynamite. They arrived with their load under tarpaulins at the Salvage Corps about 2:30 p.m. Here they

encountered a delay because the insurance men were not sure if dynamiting might invalidate insurance claims.

After a forceful talk by the Mayor, they finally agreed that if destruction of a building was authorized by the Fire Department officials, they would honor any claims. Two fire officers were designated by the mayor to select the buildings to be dynamited.

Events in the first hour of the fire occurred with such astonishing rapidity as to defy chronological order. It is evident however that the city officials, as well as the officers in charge, were quick to assess the situation and take prompt and positive action. Within three minutes of the automatic alarm, Box 447 had been pulled, and within ten more minutes the third alarm was actuated. By the time the Hurst Building fell, before 11:25 a.m., the general alarm had gone out and aid from Washington requested.

About noon, without waiting to be called, Baltimore County Engine 1 from Roland Park

Roland Park Fire Department, Roland Park, MD (in 1919, Roland Park was incorporated as part of Baltimore City)

came two miles. Engine 2 came four miles from Highlandtown, drawn by horses over the road under the command of Chief Charles Herrman.

At the 2nd Presbyterian Church, on Baltimore and Lloyd Streets, the minister dismissed the congregation due to the big fire in town. Mrs. John Bauer had returned to her home on Bond Street near Fayette and found her four daughters crowded at their bathroom window watching the fire. From their high vantage point just off Fayette St. east of Jones Falls, they could see the buildings flame up and the walls fall.

As young Joseph A. Burns, an altar boy at St. Augustine's in Elkridge left church at noon, he saw flames leaping high in the air over Baltimore, nine miles away. With his father, George Burns, they took the B&O train to Baltimore, not primarily to see the fire, but to pay their respects to a relative in South Baltimore who had passed away. When they returned to their home in St. Denis, Hose Reels #2 of St. Denis and #1 of Relay, Baltimore County, were preparing to go to the

Camden Station - B&O Railroad, Baltimore, MD

aid of Baltimore. Ropes were manned and the equipment, under the command of Chief G. N. Schaffer, was pulled to the crossing at Relay and loaded on flat cars of the B&O Railroad for the nine mile run to Camden Station. The elder Burns, and an uncle, Joseph Gillen, were members of the department and went with them, not returning until Tuesday. At the fire they connected their hose either to Baltimore engines or to fire plugs.

About 1:34 a.m., Engines 3 and 6 of the Washington, DC Fire Department arrived by special train after a thirty-eight minute dash along 40 miles of B&O rails. The equipment was carried on flat cars, the horses in cattle cars, and the men in a passenger car, with 2000 feet of extra hose in the aisle. On arrival, they moved up Howard Street to the cheers of the crowds and were ordered into position in Little Sharp Street north of Baltimore Street. Their hose did not fit the Baltimore plugs. Undaunted, they wrapped them to the plugs with canvas bandages and went to work. Here, in this

Relay Train Station, Relay, MD
Photographer: Henry Rinn, Jr.

narrow alley, ten feet curb to curb, the walls of the buildings towering above them, dense smoke and showers of sparks raining down on them, they forced their weak streams within three feet of the walls and made a determined and heroic stand.

Like many others, attracted by the passing engines and the great smoke cloud over the business district, fifteen year old Forrest Griffith and his father, after eating their mid-day dinner, hastened downtown to view the excitement. As they neared the center of the city, smoke assailed their eyes and nostrils and the din increased. One scene impressed the young man so indelibly that on his return home he drew a picture of it. Buildings were burning furiously on both sides of a narrow street, sending great clouds of smoke and showers of sparks into the street. A steamer was supplying water to firemen with hoses on the ground and on surrounding roofs as a new line was being stretched from a horse drawn hose reel. A chief, in his buggy, came to direct the operations. As they watched, they were obliged to dodge the sparks, and brush them from their clothes.

As the fire raged in Lombard Street, ex-Chief McAfee offered his services and they were accepted. With a raincoat covering his dress clothes, he recruited volunteers and directed hose streams, offering encouragement to the men. His orders were accepted without question. It was nearby, in Sharp Street, on a Sunday in 1888, that his brother Hiram, a fireman with number 7 Engine, was caught with six others beneath the collapsing walls of the Brown Drug Company, and killed.

Many other retired officers and men volunteered and rendered their services. Among them were ex-Chief Thomas J. Murphy, Captains Henry Dunn, J.J. Flynn, Lindsay and others. Special honors were later proposed for ex-Chief McAfee by friends and admirers for his services at the fire. This action was rejected by the Board of Fire Commissioners on the grounds that other ex-firemen had also rendered services.

Rather than a racing rampaging wall of flames, the fire took on the proportions of an irresistible force, sending forth huge sheets and tongues of flame. Generally it appeared to take one and one half hours to move a block, although buildings did ignite and burn several blocks beyond the main front. It was Chief Emrich's strategy to detach whatever companies he could to squash the numerous small fires started by flying sparks and brands beyond the main body of the fire. Chemical companies and ladder trucks were detailed to the outlying districts to prevent these spot fires from spreading and consolidating.

#6 Engine House-Gay Street (image taken of Engine House c. 1925. Building constructed 1853; remained virtually unchanged)

Meanwhile, employees of the City Water Department visited each engine in service to check the water supply.

Dr. Edwin Geer established a first aid station at No. 6 Engine House, Gay and Ensor Streets for the men. Many were treated for smoke inhalation, inflamed eyes, cuts, and exhaustion.

The only serious injury was that of Jacob Iglefritz, a York, PA fireman, who broke his leg getting away from a falling wall. Someone observed that the station looked like a Civil War field hospital.

Although Baltimore was a major city by all standards, it was more generally regarded as a "big town". Many of its citizens owned their homes, and there was a fierce loyalty to home, town and employer. This was an important factor in the conflagration. Realizing danger to home and livelihood, they pitched in with a will, in some instances to their individual peril. Many volunteered in the fire lines, moving hose, carrying fuel to the engines and looking after the needs of the firemen. Others saw to the protection of their homes, businesses and places of employment. Using brooms, buckets, blankets, hose lines and any other means at their disposal to extinguish the steady deluge of sparks and embers each made his personal contribution.

Businessmen and their loyal employees flocked to the area to save what they could. Any conveyance that would roll was pressed into service. At times these activities contributed to the spread of the fire as the flames entered when buildings were opened to remove their contents. Teams of horses and wagons were backed up to the curbs and crammed the streets. As they were loaded and moved away their iron tires cut the hose lines.

Jones Falls, a sizeable stream, had in earlier days meandered through the city from the north, loop-

Jones Falls: looking south from Baltimore Street toward the Harbor.
Photographer: Henry Rinn, Jr.

ing as far west as Calvert and Lexington Streets before emptying into the eastern part of the basin. Frequently flooding had occurred, the most notable being the Great Flood of July 14, 1837. At that time, water rose to 10 feet in

Jones Falls: looking west towards Burnt District.

Harrison and Frederick Streets and claimed the lives of nineteen citizens. By 1904 its path had been confined between stone walls about 100 feet apart. From Baltimore Street to City Dock five bridges spanned the stream.

To the east of the Falls lay a residential section comprised mainly of people of Italian or Jewish extraction. The area was generously dotted with large lumber yards. Their immediate protection was No. 3 Engine on East Lombard Street. It had long since crossed to the west to fight the fire, followed by 11 Engine and the Baltimore County Company from Highlandtown. Now it was up to these people to protect their own.

They took to the roofs and porches of their homes to combat the sparks and burning

23

brands that filled the air and rained down upon them. Young Robert Brotman was one. From his home east of Jones Falls at 103 South High Street, he had hurried to the center of the city to view the excitement. On his way home he stopped at the newspaper office at Baltimore and South Streets to read the bulletins among the excited crowd. Frightened, he had squeezed out of the crowd and headed home. About a block from his house he stopped to watch people dousing their roofs with buckets of water. Suddenly he became conscious of his own wooden porch and outhouse and hurried home. There was a washtub of water on the porch and his mother gave him a bucket to douse the sparks. He placed himself against the west wall for protection against the wind and cinders. Flying embers were like Fourth of July balloons. A large flaming plank fell on the porch with a tremendous thud and he put it out with a bucket of water. This post he held throughout the rest of the day,

Myer Atkins of the same area in Little Italy, had heard explosions in town and the excited shouts of neighbors as they ran to the column of smoke in the west. Donning warm clothing, he and his father followed. Watching the fire for about an hour, they noticed the burning paper and trash that was being carried over their heads by the wind and hurried home. They arrived in time to see that sparks had landed and were smoldering on the wood shingle roof of their small two-story frame house. Quickly borrowing two or three ladders from a nearby factory they placed them against the house. Rounding up all the buckets they could, his mother and sister formed a bucket brigade, filling them in the kitchen and passing them up the ladder. The sky looked like a big snowstorm - with big sparks instead of snowflakes. They kept dousing the roof until

the fire was brought under control on Monday night before getting some rest. They then left the ladder in place, and kept the buckets ready for another full day, just in case.

Esther Wilner's father (Hillman) worked for Sol Ginsberg in a factory across from the Hurst Building. That morning he came hurrying to his home on Sharp Street at Camden Street, just south of the fire, carrying enormous ledger books. Slapping them on a chair with the admonition that the children were not to bother them, he went back for more. Returning, he took his nine year old son, Sam, to help carry bolts of cloth. They kept running back and forth with the bolts until the police would not let them go back any more. The family ran upstairs and carried down all their "perenes" (eiderdown quilts) for safety. That night the children slept downstairs on the perenes while their parents poured buckets of water on the roof. Esther remembers her father on the roof and her mother on the sidewalk below, filling the bucket and tying a rope to it so the men could pull it up.

None of the firemen could go home. They would work four hours and rest one. The police came to Esther's neighborhood and asked for help. Hot coffee and shelter were needed for the firemen. A fire was built in the big Latrobe stove with wood and coal, the perenes were dragged in on the floor and there the firemen slept. Then Esther's mother began baking bread to serve the men with their coffee. Nearby merchants and neighbors, Singer and Surastky, sent groceries and dry clothes for the firemen free of charge. Mother and father worked day and night, catching a nap on a kitchen couch and keeping the stoves going. Since there were men sleeping around the clock the house had to stay quiet. It was Esther's job to watch the smaller children so they wouldn't make any noise.

The firemen were black with soot. As they washed and dried themselves on the towels, the towels turned black. Her mother would stand all day over the washboard scrubbing them clean, while her father strung lines about the kitchen to dry them on. Buckets were provided for the tired firemen's toilet and her mother carried them out to empty in the outdoor toilet and bring in the empty ones. After the firemen had left, the bare wood floors were black from soot. The family was left to scrub and clean them.

At 2:00 p.m. the guests of the Old Carrollton Hotel rushed out, bag and baggage, for safer accommodations.

Early in the afternoon, a wagon loaded with 1000 lbs. of dynamite, covered with dirt, arrived from Anne Arundel County and was parked for over an hour on Lombard Street between Hanover and Charles Streets.

George Beadenkoph, Engineer for the Consolidated Gas Company, hurried to the Gas Company building at 5-7 West Baltimore Street where he discovered the roof to be on fire. He obtained meter wagons at a Calvert Street stable and loaded company records in them with the help of other employees. With a man in the back of each wagon to beat off the sparks, he hauled the records to the company's South Street office. When the flames threatened again he moved them to Consolidated's Canton Station, shut down two weeks previous. Beadenkoph and his crew reactivated the station and went to work plugging gas mains. Those too hot to handle they plugged with globs of wet clay on the end of a length of pipe.

Fire hit the Sherwood Building on Baltimore Street so hard and fast that the iron front fell as one piece. The men of No. 9 Engine, in front of the building, escaped being crushed by crashing through a nearby store window.

It was hoped that Hanover Street, one of the city's wider streets, forty feet, might serve as a fire break. Here engines were massed and hose lines taken to the roofs and upper floors of the buildings on the east side of the street.

Old Carrollton Hotel, southeast corner of Baltimore & Light Streets

The smoke was thick and choking. The wires overhead sputtered, sizzled and burned.

Pipeman Frank A. Kraft of 17 Engine was struck over the heart by a stream of water, hurled several feet and was badly injured.

For a while, it looked as though the firemen might succeed. But this too, was to be denied. At 3:00 p.m., 150 barrels of whiskey in the upper floors at 24 South Hanover Street erupted with a tremendous roar. Tons of debris went hurtling through the air, driving the fire to the east side of the street.

DYNAMITE!

Mayor McLane and his secretary, Harry W. Rodgers, were at Hanover and Lombard Streets when the east side of Hanover Street began to burn. With the intention of dynamiting the block bounded by Hanover, German, Charles and Lombard Streets, he ordered Deputy Marshal Farnum to drive the crowd back beyond Light Street on the east and Pratt Street on the south.

Word that dynamite was to be used spread like wildfire. In Pin Alley, behind the stores on Charles, German and Howard Streets, teamsters were moving out merchandise. As the lead wagon reached Charles Street, the driver heard the word "Dynamite!" and was terror-stricken. Panic ensued in the narrow alley as it became a tangled mass of horses, wagons and people. Police labored for one half hour to calm them and send them straight down Charles Street.

Chief Burkhardt then gave the order to dynamite Charles Street near German. Dynamiting was begun by Roy E. Lafferty, assisted by C. R. Weaver and H. A. Albert, and under the supervision of City Engineer Fendall. Fifty sticks of dynamite were placed in the basement of the Schwab Building, southeast corner of Charles and German Streets, detonators inserted, wires run, and the plunger pushed. There was a tremendous blast. Windows broke, the ground shook, but the building stood. Charges were next placed two doors to the South in John Duer and Sons and in the Armstrong Shoe Manufacturing Company, between Duer and Schwab. Flames from the fire in Hanover Street were into the rear of the buildings as the charges were placed.

In one of the buildings Flanigan and his crew of five found themselves trapped when the iron doors expanded and jammed. All first floor windows were covered with iron bars embedded in stone. Dashing to the second floor, they found a window where the bars were set in wood. These they knocked out with an axe and slid, carrying fifty pounds of dynamite, down a rope. The building was burning so fast, straws were drawn to see who would be last man.

The blast felled the Armstrong Building, but only blew out the windows in Duer's, leaving a shell. Flaming debris leapt over the remains of the Schwab Building and seized upon the lunch room of T. C. Buck, on the northwest corner of Charles and German. By now the dynamiters had gone to the north side of German Street, between Charles and Hanover Streets and set off three more charges. A seventh charge was placed in the Consolidated Gas Company on west Baltimore Street. Flames were now in the Armstrong, Cator and Company Building and Oehms Acme Hall, located at the southwest corner of Baltimore

Armstrong, Cator & Company and Oehms Acme Hall

and Charles Streets. The effort to create a fire stop was fruitless, for in a few minutes the whole block was on fire.

Number 9 Engine's steamer, a new LaFrance, was pumping at the corner of Baltimore and Charles Street late Sunday afternoon. The onslaught of the fire on Baltimore Street made it necessary to move the engine. One of the horses would not go into harness and there was no time to lose. With one horse on one side of the tongue, Engineer Daniel R. Rogers and Secretary of the Fire Board Pinkney Whyte Wilkinson yoked themselves to the other side and pulled the heavy engine two blocks up Charles Street Hill

Ruins-Guggenheimer, Weil & Company, Lithographers, Lombard & Liberty Streets; building is one block south of starting point. This was southwest limit of fire.

to Lexington Street and safety. Considering the weight of the engine and the steep grade, bystanders most certainly must have lent helping hands. In an effort to save the buildings to the east between Baltimore and Fayette Streets, two buildings east of the Mullins Hotel were blown up. Smoke in the streets was so dense, firemen could hardly find their way out. One stumbled across a bursting hose line and was injured about the face.

On Baltimore Street Captain Bernard Ward, of the Northern Police District was badly burned when his celluloid collar burst into flames from the intense heat. He then issued an order for all policemen to remove their collars. Nearby, Captain Edward Schleigh of the Fire Department shared the same experience.

At 4:00 p.m., the call for aid went out to Philadelphia. Engine 43, 21 and 11 were loaded on cars of the B&O at Twenty Fourth and Race Streets. Between then and midnight, Philadelphia had dispatched four more engines; 27, 18, 23 and 16 to the stricken city.

The progress of the fire against the wind was no less dramatic than its progress with the wind. By 4:25 p.m., Guggenheimer, Weil & Company, lithographers at Lombard and Liberty Streets, was ablaze from cellar to roof. Isaac S. George and Walter C. Sheller were among the crowd watching the blaze. Paint was peeling off the sides of the huge Lloyd L. Jackson Building, a wholesale dry goods and notions company opposite on the Southeast corner and it appeared it was sure to go. Employees of the company took blankets from the stock in the building, saturated them, and draped them over the eaves. They then plugged the roof drains and let the water from a tank on the roof flood the roof and cascade down the front of the building, thereby saving it. Finally, the wall of Guggenheimer, Weil & Company fell, carrying with it the large lithographing stones and presses, narrowly missing a chief directing operations.

Just a few blocks away at Camden Station, the B&O Railroad had sent a load of coal for the fire engines. Men and women alike were unloading the coal and carrying it in wheelbarrows to the engines. The B&O Railroad supplied numerous carloads of coal and switch engines to move the cars to desired locations along the waterfront.

By 5:00 p.m., all buildings between Hopkins Place and Liberty Street had been leveled from Baltimore Street to Lombard and the fire had reached Light Street.

Conductor Jenkins of the B&O Railroad was among those who had heard the explosion in the Hurst Building and hurried out to see what the matter was. He met hundreds on the same errand. As he approached the center of the city, fire engines began to dash past him and he saw the flames leaping skyward. Of those who flocked to the scene, many did not linger. The high wind was blowing red hot pieces of tin, burning wood, cotton sparks and other blazing objects for blocks around. People became anxious and hurried home. Embers were falling on their roofs. Men and women swarmed to their roofs with buckets and brooms to dash away the sparks. Many house-tops and awnings were set afire. Householders quickly extinguished these small blazes as they realized they could expect no aid from the fire companies battling the blaze in the heart of the city. Cinders and sparks fell upon them, blacking their faces and burning holes in their clothes. Many dropped to their knees and prayed that their homes would be spared.

Before leaving Baltimore with his train at 6:00 o'clock, Conductor Jenkins went up into the dome at Camden Station three blocks from the fire. Although the wind was blowing in the opposite direction, he could feel the heat and hear the roar of the flames and the crash of falling walls.

The heat was so intense, in many places the firemen were unable to approach the flames close enough to train their hose streams on the fire. They had to resort to soaking the surrounding buildings in an effort to keep them from catching fire.

James Thompson of New York, a traveling salesman, left the Carrollton House to catch the 6:00 a.m. train. Looking up Hanover Street, on his way to the station, he witnessed an unforgettable spectacle. A wall of flames and smoke rose hundreds of feet into the air. The heat beat against his face like looking into a furnace. Now and then the wind would sweep the smoke aside to present a scene of tottering walls and twisted iron girders. The air was thick with showers of cinders, and pieces of burning wood and hot tin. At 6:00 p.m., the fire was still raging with equal intensity within a one block radius of its origin as it was at its northeastern limits. The southwestern sector, bounded by Howard and Lombard Streets, was not contained until late Sunday afternoon. During this time the fire had worked its way down the east side of Liberty Street to Lombard. Crossing Liberty Street to the west, it set fire to John R. Edwards Bindery and Gaither's Express on the corner of Lombard and Howard Streets. As J. J. Harris and Company at 40 South Howard Street began to burn in the upper floor, Lieutenant Frederick W. Johnston of No. 4 truck had his men lower him over the edge of the roof on a rope with a line of hose. Breaking the windows with the nozzle, he directed a stream of water on the flames, extinguishing them and saving the building.

At Howard and German Streets, F. A. Davis and Co., tobacco and cigars burned. The Café Howard, at 17 North Howard Street, owned by Thomas Agnew, caught fire twice during the afternoon, was checked by the firemen, but badly damaged by water. Here, the efforts of the firemen were successful in confining the fire to its western limit. Meanwhile, the progress of the fire to the north and east continued unabated. Having crossed Hanover Street and Baltimore Street, it now was working its way north to Fayette Street.

At the northeast corner of Fayette and Liberty Streets, as Lineman William H. Moffitt was cutting wires of the United Railways and Electric Co., he received a shock from a live wire and was thrown from the pole and injured. He was taken to City Hospital in a Central District ambulance.

United Railway & Electric Company, or Pratt Street Power House, looking west.

Brick walls and fire shutters in the new United Railways and Electric Company's Transformer Station at 6 - 8 McClellan Alley helped save half the block. Here again, at 114 - 124 W. Fayette Street, the building of Oppenheimer, Obendorf and Co. was saved by employees who kept the roof wet down by use of a private hose line. Crawling out on a balcony over the first floor windows, they wet down the front of the building and spectators too. Although the building was sprinklered, the sprinklers were not activated. Next door, Wise Brothers also was spared, as well as Gans Brothers.

From here, the fire worked its way east along Fayette St., burning J. J. Jenkins Company just west of Charles Street. On the southwest corner of Charles and Fayette stood J. W. Putts and Company, a four story building with large glass front and side windows. On being asked if he were agreeable to having his building dynamited to halt the flames, Mr. Putts reply was "Sure — blow it up if it will do any good." It didn't. Instead it drove the fire into Headington and Hall on the northwest corner and shattered the windows in the Union Trust Building on the northeast corner.

The Union Trust was a modern, steel-framed ten-story building. Flames from the blazing Headington and Hall Building crossed Charles St. and entered Union Trust. It was the first of the fireproof skyscrapers in the city to go. The masonry was destroyed and the building gutted. However, the basic protected steel structure withstood the test. After the fire, the dam-

O'Neill's Department Store corner of Charles and Lexington Streets, looking southwest. Shows original row house structure and three other buildings added on. Mr. O'Neill had store signs repainted just after the fire as his building was one of the few landmarks still standing.

aged masonry was cleared and the building rebuilt within the year.

With the intersection of Charles and Fayette Streets fully involved, and the fire moving north and east, it was planned to dynamite the O'Neill Building at Charles and Lexington. O'Neill's, the fashionable premier ladies wear and dry goods store stood at the highest topographical point of the fire. A large brick building, it faced on Charles and Lexington Streets and was bounded on the west by Crooked Lane. This narrow winding alley was a remnant of the Great Eastern Road that George Washington had traveled. The blank south wall of the building adjoined the blazing building of Slessinger's Shoe Store and Headington and Hall.

Now the officials wanted to dynamite it. Thomas O'Neill, the owner, would have no part of it. Planting himself squarely within his building, he declared that if they did, they would blast him too. As he would not budge, they had to desist. The suggestion was then made to blow the Fidelity Building, an eight story granite structure across Lexington Street on the northwest corner. Mayor McLane, among those present, declared that the building would not be dynamited.

In the meantime, O'Neill and his employees busied themselves to save their building. The windows facing on Crooked Lane were protected by 113 sprinklers supplied by the city mains. They were turned on and kept in operation from 5:15 p.m. to 8:15 p.m. Fifteen sprinkler heads in the attic activated due to the roof boards ignited from the hot tin roof above. There, employees labored in confined spaces preventing the fire from spreading, saving the store and halting the spread of the fire to the north. O'Neill, a devout Catholic, hurried to the Cathedral to pray and vowed that if his building was saved he would provide

Rear of O'Neill's Department Store after the Fire. Shown are a police officer and two gentlemen in bowler hats (possibly detectives).

a new cathedral. From the bequest of Thomas O'Neill, the Cathedral of Mary Our Queen was dedicated in November 1959 on North Charles Street. O'Neill is immortalized in one of its stained glass windows and a panel depicting the fire forms part of an altar.

As darkness began to fall, the scene from the roof of the Belvedere Hotel on North Charles Street was one of terrifying magnificence. As the flames and smoke billowed, the figure of George Washington atop the monument glowed in silhouette. One observer made the remark, *"The father of our country looks like Nero gloating over the destruction of Rome."* His companion replied, *"All he needs is a fiddle."*

Fireboat "Cataract" at Engine Company #16, located at Commercial Wharf, south of Thames Street in Fells Point (after 1897).

About 6:00 p.m., Police Commissioner Upshur requested General Lawreson Riggs to call out units of the Maryland National Guard to assist the police. The City Hall bell "Big Sam" was tolled three times, repeatedly; the signal for assembly.

About 7:00 p.m., the fireboat "Cataract" had been moved up to Pratt and Light Streets to help fight the fire in the area at German and Liberty where it was burning as fiercely at 6:00 p.m. as when it began. Two thousand feet of hose was stretched to German Street. Before it could be used it was cut to ribbons by the tires of wagons, as merchants and businessmen struggled to salvage what they might in the face of the flames.

Businessmen, called from their homes by watchmen and police, began removing their valuables. A jeweler, on hearing of the fire, like other merchants, had hurried to his establishment to save what he could. As the flames approached, he labored feverishly to open his safe. In the excitement, the combination eluded him and his fingers fumbled as they turned the dial. His faithful employees, hovering anxiously over him, offered advice and assistance. At last his efforts were rewarded; the door came open. At this crucial juncture came the dull realization that there was no means to move the wares. Turning to his young office boy, Gus (Babe) Baumgartner, he said *"Babe, get me a dray"*. With any means of transportation at premium, Babe took off in search. Running up Charles Street, the only conveyance he could find was a horse drawn hearse and driver parked in front of the Masonic Temple. On trying to engage the vehicle, he was told by the driver that he was awaiting funeral services in the temple. In some manner Babe was able to persuade the driver to go with him. The jeweler's fortune was transported to safety in a hearse. How the deceased fared is lost to time.

The fire in the block bounded by Charles, Lexington, Fayette and St. Paul Streets did not burn as fiercely or swiftly as it did in the block to the south. Here, the flames moved swiftly east, between Fayette and Baltimore Streets toward St. Paul Street. On the east side, at 7 St. Paul Street, stood the Central Telephone Exchange. Miss Anne Schmidt, a supervisor, described the drama within. As darkness began to fall and the fire approached, the blinds had to be drawn against the glare to enable the operators to distinguish the signal lights on their switchboards. Approximately forty operators were on duty. Sparks and burning embers landed on the window sills and roof, as firemen played streams on the building. As it grew hotter, the girls were swathed in wet blankets against the heat. At about 6:13 p.m., the flames broke through on the west side of the block at the Daily Record Building. Windows in the Telephone Exchange began to crack from the heat. It became impossible for the operators to continue.

Beginning with the operators on the top floor, the girls filed out in formation carrying their headsets, assisted by firemen at each landing. They passed through an interconnecting passage to the Calvert Building and thence to Fayette Street. Here, waiting police escorted them to Gay Street. By 8:00 p.m., the Exchange was gutted. The operators were then escorted to exchanges north of the fire zone. Among them, were Marie and Annie Winkler. They fled before they could gather up their purses. They worked the phones from another exchange, sleeping on cots provided by the National Guard. A man from the telephone company went to their home at North and Gay Streets and got suitcases of clothes for both girls. It was three weeks before they returned home.

32

At 7:00 p.m., the wind changed to 25 mph from the west, and was blowing the fire like a whirlwind straight down Lombard, German, Baltimore and Fayette Streets.

Daily Record Building at St. Paul and Fayette Streets

As preparations were being made to dynamite the Daily Record Building on the southwest corner of St. Paul and Fayette Streets, Judge Henry D. Harlan rushed up to Chief Burkhardt and told him, *"If you destroy that building, Baltimore will be doomed. Concussion will break every window in the Court House"*. As they talked, men in the Court House could be seen with buckets and hoses trying to keep the windowsills and frames from catching fire. With the fire about a half block away, Harlan convinced Burkhardt, and the Record Building was not dynamited.

Flanigan, the dynamiter, was ordered to remove the dynamite. Carrying the box of dynamite on his shoulder, he was walking east on Fayette Street past the Court House when he discovered a fist-sized burning ember in the box. His reaction was immediate and swift. Setting the box down, he ran to the corner of Fayette & Calvert before even looking back. The dynamite was burning like sawdust, but never did explode. The only explanation he could offer was that due to the extremely cold night, the powder might have been frozen.

As the fire was working its way east along Fayette St., the Sisters of Mercy, who conducted the City Hospital, realized that an evacuation might be required and made preparations. Each of the 300 or more patients were quietly notified of the possibility and arrangements were made with Maryland General Hospital, Johns Hopkins University, the Maryland University and St. Joseph's Hospitals. Early in the afternoon, eighteen female patients, two babies and seven nurses were taken from the Maryland Maternity and Laying-In Hospital on Lombard Street, west of

Hanover, and transported in patrol wagons to City Hospital on Calvert Street near Saratoga.

Mrs. Christine Kludsekaulke who was ill with typhoid, with her two small children, on the opposite side of the street at 100 West Lombard, was taken out by Patrolman Smith and also sent to City Hospital. Soon after, flames from the blazing Anchor Shirt Company jumped across Lombard Street, setting fire to the Laying-In Hospital which was partially saved by means of private hose lines from the roof of North Brothers and Straus & Company's building on the corner below. A few minutes after the removal of the Kludzekaulke family, the five story Anchor Shirt Building next door fell with a crash. Three of the stories crashed through the roof of No. 100 and took two other buildings with them.

On South Charles Street the Baker Glass Company caught fire. Shortly after, a tremendous explosion lifted the roof ten feet in the air and blew it across the street, striking the front of the burning Smith Dixon Building. Nearby on Light Street, hardware employees removed a supply of dynamite from their store and spread it in the street so the powder would be dampened in the mud and not go off.

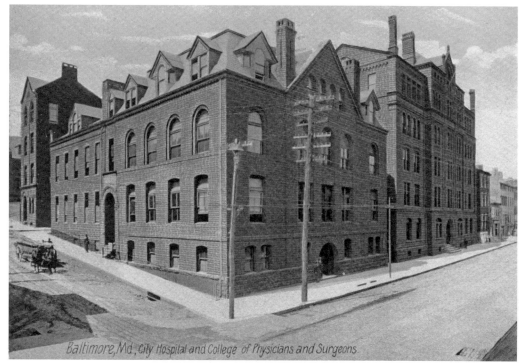

Baltimore, Md., City Hospital and College of Physicians and Surgeons.

Postcard of City Hospital, Lombard Street

Between 7:00 and 8:00 p.m., Miss Emma Burke was summoned to open a safe on the top floor of the Equitable Building and save $10,000 in bonds in a lawyers office where she was employed. When she reached the building it was deserted. The excitement was intense. The strain on the young lady's nerves was too much, and at the sixth floor she displayed signs of distress. She was faint, but she told the two young men who accompanied her not to give up, and if they would carry her she would be all right by the time they reached the office. The men were determined, and lost no time in picking the young woman up and struggled up the two remaining flights with their feminine burden. Once inside the office, Miss Burke soon regained her composure to the extent that she was able to open the safe and get the bonds. Shortly afterwards, the rear of the Equitable Building caught fire.

District Engineer No. 6 E. Louis Shipley was heard to remark, *"A thousand fire companies cannot stop it, the fire is king tonight."*

At 8:30 in the evening the roof of the Zion Church caught fire in two places. Two members of the church climbed along the steep ridge of the roof and extinguished the flames with buckets of water before the engines arrived. The precautions of the congregation saved not only the church and school, but aided in preventing extension of the fire to the east in that area.

Also at 8:30, the Annapolis Rescue Hose, Water Witch Hook and Ladder, and Engine 2 arrived over the B&A Railroad under the command of Assistant Chief Phillip E. Porter. Their couplings would not fit those of the city,

Junkers Hotel, Fayette Street

so they were assigned to draft from the docks along Pratt Street.

From the blazing Union Trust at Lafayette and Charles, the buildings on the north side of Fayette went. The Junkers Hotel in the middle of the block burned, then Lemmert's Tailors. On the corner of St. Paul, the seven-story Daily Herald, H. L. Mencken's paper, was abandoned and the young city editor was forced to flee. On the south side of Fayette Street, Saunders and Staymans Music Store was dynamited, but the flames soon consumed the debris. In the middle of the block Muth's Wholesale Chemical Company burned, the chemicals within exploding with great violence. At the corner, the Daily Record Building went, with flames jumping St. Paul Street to the Calvert Building.

From the Telephone Exchange also, the fire entered the Calvert Building, another steel-

Photographer Henry Rinn, Jr.

Bird's Eye View of U.S. Post Office, taken from roof of City Hall

framed skyscraper, directly across from the United States Post Office. The Post Office, a castellated red brick edifice, occupied the full block on Fayette Street from St. Paul to Calvert. Wind direction and efforts of the firemen kept the fire to the south side of Fayette St. where it entered the nine story Equitable Building, a huge steel and red tile building, extending down the hill along Fayette St. fronting on Calvert. This building occupied almost one quarter of the square block. Earlier, George L. Radcliffe, a young attorney later to become a long-time United States Senator, culminated a long strenuous afternoon of removing files by saving a 35 lb. bronze statue of a lion. This relic he was able to display

years later on his desk, as his personal reminder of the Great Fire.

About dusk, engine and men from Altoona, PA, arrived at Calvert Station. Fireman George Potter recalls vividly, *"What we saw when we got off the train made us want to go home to Altoona. The air was so thick with smoke it seemed like midnight. You could hear the noise of the fire. You could smell it. That everything around us was strange (none of us had been to Baltimore before) made it all the worse.*

We hitched up and headed downtown. There, fire engines were clattering to and fro. Men, wet and grimy and red-eyed, were stumbling through the streets with the hoses. It was the worst sight I've ever seen.

We were ordered to Fayette Street, near the Post Office, to play water on an office building that was ablaze. We unhitched the horses, which were lead out of the danger area until we would need them again; we unlimbered our hose and set to work. Bricks and embers fell all around us, and the earth shook; the city was dynamiting some buildings.

By the middle of that cold night, the boys' eyes were so puffed up and inflamed from the smoke that they had difficulty in seeing; some of them were returned to the train at the station for treatment. All the boys were wet to the skin — even though they were wearing rubber suits.

A few times during the night someone came down from the train with hot coffee and sandwiches, and that did a lot to help us. Some visiting firemen relieved their discomfort by breaking into saloons and appropriating the stock. Not our boys though — Billy

Irvin and Ike Long had warned us on the train that they expected us to uphold our city's good name.

We all thought the fire would get the Courthouse and City Hall. Then, about midnight the wind shifted and took the flames South. We followed. I remember that we hitched up and went down to a cannery that was burning on Jones' Falls".

South of the Equitable Building and behind the Telephone Exchange, across a narrow alley known as Bank Lane, the flames took possession of the central offices of the B&O Railroad, a monumental structure. An attempt was made to dynamite it, but only a part of one wall fell, firing the adjoining building on Baltimore Street. Catercorner from the B&O,

Photographer Henry Rinn, Jr.

Continental Trust Building, Baltimore & Calvert Streets; at 14 stories, this was Baltimore's tallest building in 1904.

the fourteen story Continental Trust, the city's tallest skyscraper took fire in the top floor. This modern structure burned like a torch from top to bottom within ten to twelve minutes. Cast iron radiators and typewriter frames within the building oxidized but did not melt. Heat from the burning skyscraper cracked every window in the Maryland Trust Company, on the northwest corner of Calvert and German, glass clattering to the street. The tall, narrow structure was brilliantly illuminated from within as if by electric lights turned on

simultaneously. At the height of the fire in this area, the flames reached an estimated temperature of 2500 – 2800 degrees F. The burning skyscrapers were visible from afar; on the Eastern Shore, to crews on ships down the bay, and to Ruth Bowers in Frederick, some forty miles away.

Mercantile Trust & Deposit Company, (behind ruins)

As the Continental Building burned, heavy-sash weights fell through a large skylight in the roof of the one story building of the Mercantile Trust and Deposit Company adjoining on the south. Burning brands and flame followed, burning out the interior.

At 9:00 p.m., Mayor McLane climbed the narrow stairs to the dark cupola of the City Hall to sound the riot call, summoning the militia. Buildings on Fayette Street were blazing so he connected the wires, causing the bell to sound continuously.

About 10:00 p.m. evacuation of City Hospital began as planned. Ambulances from the hospitals previously contacted and the Police Department, as well as regimental ambulances, began to remove the patients. The more critical patients were completely covered so they could not see what was happening. Those able to walk climbed into the ambulances, while others were carried on stretchers. All personal belongings were packed and carried to the Calvert St. entrance. For two hours the ambulances were busy transporting the patients. Meanwhile, physicians of the hospital staff, stationed on the roof, extinguished the cinders that fell.

Philadelphia Engine Companies Numbers 11, 21, and 43 arrived at 10:05 p.m. under command of Assistant Chief Edward A. Waters. Engine 43's couplings were compatible with Baltimore, the other two companies being assigned to the waterfront at Pratt and Light Streets. Their positioning was to play a critical part in the battle.

Governor Edwin Warfield

At 10:15 p.m. Governor Edwin Warfield arrived at Camden Station from Annapolis.

About 11:00 p.m. Sunday, winds moderated to fourteen miles per hour from the northwest and held this direction into early Monday morning.

The Carrollton Hotel at German and Light burst into flames around midnight and soon was ablaze from cellar to roof. Behind the Carrollton, the Maryland Trust, on the northwest corner of German and Calvert blazed up. As it burned and the walls fell, a portion of the debris fell on the roof of Alex. Brown & Sons, a one-story building on the southwest corner of Baltimore and Charles. As the skyscrapers at this intersection burned, the greatest heat of the fire was generated, reaching an estimated 2800 degrees F. Perhaps due in part to the fact

Maryland Institute - after the Fire

that Alex. Brown & Sons was surrounded by blazing skyscrapers creating a flue above, and to the insulating effect of the debris on the roof, the building was spared.

As the fire burned furiously in the skyscrapers at Baltimore and Calvert Streets, flying brands set fire to the roof of the Maryland Institute, five blocks to the east. Fronting on Baltimore Street and extending south down Marsh Market to Water Street, the Maryland Institute Association of Mechanical Arts was a landmark. Built in 1848, the street floor housed Center Market. The hall above, at the time, was the largest hall in America under

Marsh Market - before the Fire

had lain in state in 1858, on the occasion of the building of their memorial in Ashland Square. It now lay in an area of decline, surrounded by smaller buildings. To the east, across West Falls Ave. lay the Jones Falls and the residential area of East Baltimore.

With all companies fighting the main body of the fire to the west there were no engines to spare. It was here that a group of veterans of the old volunteer department, members of the Veterans Volunteer Firemens' Association, went into action. Under the direction of their president, Augustus Albert, they dragged their hose reels out of the Pioneer Hook and Ladder House at No. 9 in Harrison Street and took a plug in front of Thomas

one clear spanned roof. Both ends of the building were capped by large cupolas; the one at Baltimore Street being a

Marsh Market - after the Fire

clock tower. It had hosted Democratic Conventions in 1856 and 1860, and had been the center for artistic and social functions. Lincoln

Sadler's Drugstore, N.E. corner of Harrison & Baltimore Streets; later relocating to another in front of their headquarters in Harrison Street.

With the burning of the Institute, the smaller buildings along Marsh Market went too. The burning of this area, in advance of the main body of the fire, provided a fire break, and was an important factor in the control of the conflagration. It was three quarters of an hour before the regulars could offer assistance in the form of a steamer in Harrison Street. With the help of the old timers, the fire was confined to the south side of Baltimore Street at this point.

Marsh Market - after the Fire

had spoken here in 1864, as well as Jenny Lind and Henry Ward Beecher. Here also, the young heroes of 1814, Wells and McComas,

Meanwhile, the flames advanced unabated down Baltimore Street. By 11:45 p.m. the American Building on the southwest corner of Baltimore and South Streets was ablaze. Directly across

Sun Iron Building, c. 1880

South Street stood the five-story Sun Iron Building, the first iron building in the country. The flames lashed out from the American Building and fired the fourth floor of the Sun Iron Building, but were extinguished and it was felt that the building might stand. At midnight, however, the flames jumped South Street in full fury and soon the fourth and fifth floors were ablaze. Within five minutes the heavy machinery on the upper floors began to fall, crashing through to the basement. At 12:30 a.m. the cast iron walls fell.

Two smaller buildings, adjoining to the south, also burned, but the Safe Deposit and Trust Company, across a narrow 10 ft. alley was spared. Immediately to the south the Commerce and Farmers National Bank, as well as the remainder of the block, fell prey to the flames.

At midnight, and into the early morning hours, as the conflagration raged at Baltimore and South Streets, it was also working its way north and east of Fayette and Charles Streets at a much slower pace. Flames took the four- and five-story buildings along the east side of

Sun Iron Building - after the Fire

Charles north of the blazing Union Trust Building and threatened the five story Central Savings Bank at Charles and Lexington Streets. Here again, with no help available, several employees labored long and hard in the attic with a small hose and buckets of water at the windows. They were successful in preventing the fire from spreading below the attic and the building was saved.

Circling around behind the bank building, the fire next hit the smaller four story buildings along the south side of Lexington Street. On the southwest corner of Lexington and St. Paul, the Law Building took fire in the top floor and the second floor below it. Flames roared from both floors before the floor between caught fire. As it did, all floors above the first lit

Law Building

off. Next door, the Condon Building was also blazing. Great tongues of flame lashed out across the narrow, twenty-foot width of St. Paul Street and attacked the Court House. Assistant Superintendent of Public Buildings Miller had stationed patrols throughout the building to keep fires from entering through the windows. He and his men worked on the roof until driven off by the heat. In the Bar Library in the northwest corner of the building, Chief Judge Harlan of the Superior Court, along with James P. Kines and others took up the battle to save the valuable collection of

Church of the Messiah - before the Fire

books and paintings. Drapes were removed from the windows, and all papers, etc. were removed to safer areas within the building. Taking a hose line, they fought the fire for hours and won. Although a number of window frames and sashes were burned out, and the marble exterior on the northwest corner was badly damaged, the Court House was saved.

While the battle to save the Court House was being waged, another battle was in progress across Lexington St. to the north, at the corner of Courtland St., to save the Maryland Telephone Building. President George R. Webb and his Assistant, a Mr. Evans, had made similar preparations. Hose and chemical extinguishers were placed on each floor. The thick walls became so hot that the

heat was felt inside. Water was turned on, and the hoses directed out the windows to cascade down the western face of the building. The walls and window frames were thoroughly saturated. When there was time, the streams were played on the waxed ends of the electric wires where they entered the building.

From the streets below, General John Hood, president of United Railways, and general manager, Mr. William A. House, who had earlier been driven from their offices in the Continental Building, watched.

The determined efforts of these men, the firemen, and a favorable wind confined the flames to the south side of Fayette Street east of St. Paul. Climaxing a long, hard struggle, the magnificent municipal buildings on the north side of the street, the Court House, United States Post Office and the City Hall were saved.

To the east, the fire continued unabated to the Church of the Messiah at the southwest corner of Gay and Fayette Streets. Although the walls and huge cupola stood, the interior was totally destroyed. Here again the flames

Messiah - during the Fire; awning frames remain to left; church can be seen through smoke at rear.

were stayed. The fire moved down the west side of Gay Street, jumping to the east side, halfway down the block, to attack the Gay

Messiah - after the Fire

Messiah during cleanup

Street Theater. Next was Habliston's Drugstore and several other businesses, in the five story building that extended along the north side of Baltimore Street almost to Frederick Street. From here the flames were confined to the south side of Baltimore Street as far as the Jones Falls.

In the early hours of Monday morning, additional aid began to arrive from other communities. Just after midnight, Chief John K. Hardy and his men of Volunteer Fire Company No. 1 from Sparrows Point, MD, ten miles away, arrived by trolley car and went to work with the Baltimore companies. Reliance No. 2 and Weccacoe No. 8 from Wilmington, DE; Engine 7 from Washington, DC; and the Laurel and Vigilant companies from York, PA arrived within an hour, followed by Hanley No. 1 and Fenton No. 3 from Chester, PA, and Hope Engine from Harrisburg, PA, Philadelphia Engines No. 18 and No. 23 arrived over the Pennsylvania Railroad. Only the two companies from York were able to connect to the Baltimore hydrants. Hope Engine from Harrisburg lashed its suction to a hydrant and went to work. All other companies took suction from the basin.

At 3:00 a.m., the Lutheran Church at Broadway and Canton Avenue caught fire from flying embers, but was saved. The merchants along Broadway began to move their wares to safety. Mr. Wigley, owner of a music store, was among them. Among other items he carried out on the sidewalk was a large cash register. When it became evident the area would be spared he went to carry the register back. Try as he might, he could not lift it.

By early morning, Fells Point was in panic. As the merchants began removing their goods to be carted to safety, men, women, and children rushed to the Broadway ferry to cross to

Maltby House, Pratt Street

Locust Point. The crowds were uncontrollable and had to be turned away. Many went to St. Stanislaus Catholic Church at Ann and Aliceanna Streets to pray for deliverance.

41

At Charles and Lombard Streets, the young volunteer firemen from Relay and St. Denis, about twenty-five in number, battled heroically to keep the flames from crossing Charles Street. Time and again they drove them back to the cheers of the crowds. But success was denied them. Despite their heroic efforts, at 3:00 a.m. the flames crossed to the east of Charles and Lombard. Here the fire continued east between Lombard and Balderson Street, a narrow street running east and west between Charles and Light. On Charles Street, south of Balderson, the flames were checked but continued to burn furiously, feeding on the stores of oils and chemicals in the warehouses lining the south side of Lombard Street. By 3:30 a.m. Monday, the area west of Charles Street and north of Lombard

Anderson & Ireland Hardware Store, Pratt & Light Streets

Street was practically burned out. East of Charles and south of Lombard the fire was still spreading, and by 4:00 a.m. was in possession of the north side of Pratt Street almost to the Falls.

Engine 16 from Philadelphia and a company from Phoenixville, PA, arrived at this time and were dispatched by Chief Emrich to the east side of the Falls, along with whatever companies were available to keep the flames from establishing a foothold on the east side.

Captain Kahl and his men had fought the fire doggedly, step by step, building by building, from the very beginning, as it worked its way slowly south against the wind. Now, between 4:00 and 5:00 a.m. Monday, still in

dress uniforms, begrimed and bedraggled, they prepared to keep the flames in Balderson Street from entering the rear of the Maltby House, a large hotel, and firing Pratt Street. Taking a hose line, they entered the building and advanced it to the rear windows. Hardly had they placed themselves in position when the building was completely involved in flame. They had to abandon the line and run for their lives as they had twenty-four hours before in the Hurst Building. With the firing of the Maltby House, the flames burst onto West Pratt Street.

Roaring east, flames attacked the hardware business of Anderson and Ireland on the corner at Pratt and Light. In the basement of this narrow three story building a large supply of explosives was stored. Hose lines were

Anderson & Ireland-after

concentrated and maintained throughout the fire to prevent another explosion. The building and fallen wires were encased in ice from the streams of water.

Kahl and his men were then ordered to hitch their horses and approach the fire from the east. To do this they were obliged to proceed up Howard Street to Center Street, then east to East Falls Avenue, and south to the waterfront.

Around midnight, the wind had changed from the west to northwest. With a velocity of fourteen mph it drove the flames south through the financial district toward East Pratt Street and the Falls. Among the buildings to go were the National Bank of Commerce, the four-story Commercial and Farmers Bank, and at South and Water Streets, the six-story spired building of the Firemen's Insurance Company. The United States Customs House under construction on Gay Street between Water and Lombard was completed up to the second floor of its projected four stories. The scaffolding was burned and the granite facing chipped. Stone stored in the street was badly damaged.

Across Exchange Place, on the southwest corner, fire entered Public Store House No. 1 through the monitor housing on the roof, over the stairs and elevator. Feeding on an old wooden hoist, it broke through to the third floor of the four story building and consumed the entire stock of bonded spirits stored there. Silks, laces and textiles on the fourth floor were not damaged. The Fire Department was able to contain the fire to the third floor.

The Merchants National Bank at the southeast corner of German and Holliday was among the last to go. Until the very last moment, a group of the bank's employees had stood in the vestibule, watching the progress of the flames. Now, forced by the firemen to leave, each bent and kissed the granite blocks forming the doorway and retreated several blocks where they stood to *see the last of her*.

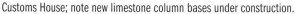

Customs House; note new limestone column bases under construction.

ALONG THE WATERFRONT

At the Falls, a peculiar shift of the wind sent the flames roaring west along both sides of Pratt Street. At 4:30 a.m., fire hit the roof of the north engine house of the United Railways Power Company. As the roof collapsed and the walls fell, the generators within stopped running, and with them all the streetcars in town. Passengers and crews were marooned. Wives and children brought the crews of the streetcars their meals. The north boiler house and the south boiler house escaped the wrath of the flames, the four tall stacks atop the south boiler house standing to this day as silent sentinels along the waterfront.

Hanley Fire Company, of Chester, PA, was among those companies fighting the fire in Pratt Street near Light. Their President, W. P. Ladomus describes the action. *"Our location was changed once. We were not ordered to leave Pratt Street, but had to; it was a furnace of fire. For hours we could hardly see on account of the rain of sparks and cinders. We had to leave our steamer for a short time on account of the terrific heat. Everything was hot (the buildings, pavement, air, street, and in fact, the water we pumped was hot). It looked for a time as if we would have to leave the engine to its fate, but by an act of Providence the wall of one of the big buildings fell completely blocking the street with bricks, and burning timbers fell each side of it."* This was probably the five-story Franklin House on the southwest corner of Pratt and Calvert. *"The men had to run for their lives, but returned in a few minutes and bravely went to work tossing bricks and timber out of the way, working only as men placed in a*

United Railway Power Station

situation of that kind can. Engine Company 27 of Philadelphia, stationed at the corner of Pratt and Light Street, seeing the danger of men and steamer, turned their stream on us until we succeeded in getting away. Hundreds of feet of hose were burned here. The fireboat rendered great aid to all the companies here by playing streams over them when they were trying to get their steamers off the dock. We then took our steamer to the hydrant at the corner of Light and Camden Streets, but could not make connection as our threads were different. This gave us a rest for about half an hour, and it was a Godsend to us, as most of us were blind from spices, pepper and cinders that filled the air. Some of the men had to be taken to the hospital for treatment.

We were then ordered to Jones Falls along with many other Companies to try and keep the flames from crossing into East Baltimore."

The Altoona Company was also dispatched to the same area. Fireman George Potter continues. *"Sometime the next morning, I think, we were transferred to a lumber yard closer to the harbor. I remember that because the*

44

water pressure was getting so low in the hydrants we put the hoses in the Falls. We worked in that area until the latter part of the afternoon, when it was apparent the fire was well under control.

Early that evening we staggered back to Calvert Station. A railroad doctor was there to treat our eyes; there was a hot meal, and dry warm clothes. After we ate, we fell into those bunks and slept like rocks. The next day we went back home."

E. Pratt Street Piers-before the Fire

Light Street was the main artery to the thickly populated residential area south of the Basin known locally as South Baltimore. From Pratt Street south for some four blocks, the basin was obscured by covered wooden loading docks, rising to two stories in places. Wagons and drays thronged the street, backed up to these docks to load or unload. The basin side of the structure provided sixteen finger piers for the bay steamers to nose into dock. Across the narrow confines of the street (forty feet) there were tall rows of commission houses and warehouses. If Light Street went, the fire would carry to South Baltimore. Around Federal Hill, a horseman rode through the neigh-

borhood, warning the residents of impending danger. At Pratt and Light Streets the Philadelphia firemen of Engines 11 and 23 were ready. At the Ericsson Line pier they gave battle. Along the Light Street piers, the flames severely damaged the Old Bay Line pier at Barre Street before being controlled. By their action in this crucial area, the commission houses along Light Street south of Pratt Street, the area to the west, and South Baltimore were spared.

For years, the waters in the southwest corner of the basin had entrapped the debris of the harbor, interfering with the docking of the steamers. It had been proposed to dig a canal along Lee Street to Sharp, and down Sharp Street to the Middle Branch of the Patapsco to relieve this condition but it was overruled. Now, the basin was covered with debris from the fire as the piers along Pratt Street began to burn. The steamer "City of Norfolk" of the Old Bay Line arrived about this time with a cargo of live chickens in crates from the Eastern

E. Pratt Street Piers-after the Fire

Shore. Due to the fire, she was diverted to Light Street and the crated chickens hastily unloaded onto the street. On Light Street, one Mushroom Murray, of 123 East Welcome Alley, grabbed a chicken and ran. To escape pursuit,

45

West Pratt Street Piers - before the Fire

Photographer Henry Rinn, Jr.

Waterfront with floating ice and debris

he ran down Quay Alley, which dead ended at the harbor. He fell into the water and drowned.

Stopped at Light Street, the flames now reversed to the east with renewed fury and attacked the Pratt Street Piers. Pratt Street, like Light was a major thoroughfare, being the direct route between the President Street Railroad Station on the east and Camden Station to the West. It was along this street that the first casualties of the Civil War had fallen. Eastward along Pratt Street there were six long wharves between Light Street and Jones Falls. Each wharf and dock reflected the identity of the city's prominent merchants. From Cheapside east there was Bowley's Wharf and McClure Dock, Patterson's/Spears Wharf and Frederick Dock, O'Donnell's/Dugan's Wharf and Long Dock, McElderry's/Union Wharf and Union Dock, Chase's Wharf and West Falls Avenue and Jones Falls.

West Falls Avenue extended some 2000 feet into the basin and made an abrupt turn eastward into Block Street. Here, at City Dock, it connected with Fell's Point via the Block Street Drawbridge. Streets on these wharves were crowded with substantial commercial buildings of every description. There were warehouses, flour mills, commission houses, offices, tobacco warehouses, lumber yards, coal yards, ship and railroad terminals, canneries, an ice house, bars and on one, the huge main powerhouse of the street railway system. In short, each wharf was a complete segment of the city unto itself.

At 6:00 a.m., the Merchants Fruit Exchange on Bowley's Wharf was

11:30 a.m., Monday the 8th-Bowley's Wharf; foot of West Falls Avenue where fire was stayed.

ablaze; flames along Wood Street jumped McClure's Dock to fire Hubbard and Company on Patterson Dock. The "Altoona", a new Amoskeag steamer commanded by Chief William Irwin, arrived at this time to protect Pennsylvania Railroad property. It had made a record run of 217 miles from Altoona, PA, by rail, the longest distance traveled by any company at the fire. Lashed to a plug, it went to work for the first time. As the fire was burning through the piers at 8:00 a.m., flames were still raging in the reading room in the rear of the Church of the Messiah at Fayette and Gay Streets.

As the buildings of the fruit exchanges of Lanosa and United Fruit on Bowley's Wharf began to burn, the tugs "Oriole" and "Meta" arrived and took the fruit steamers "Avalon", "Trold" and "Bodo" in tow. Returning, they were able to move the steamer "Hippolyte Damois", at the Digiorgio Dock, to safety as the flames approached to a point less than 100 feet away from the ship.

On the extreme end of Bowley's Wharf, at 9:00 a.m., Reliance No. 2 and Weccacoe No. 8 from Wilmington, DE, were fighting the flames in a wooden structure of the Baltimore, Chester and Atlantic Railway Company. They were cut off by an explosion in the Standard Oil Warehouse at the corner of Pratt Street and rescued by tugboats. Fifteen minutes later the wind changed long enough for them to be put ashore and to rush in and secure their badly damaged engine. Within a few more minutes the wharf was a mass of

flames. The crew of the Fenton Engine No. 3, also from Chester, was caught on a pier and had to run through the flames in order to escape, barely missing being caught by a falling wall.

To save the books of C.A. Gambrill's Manufacturing Company's flour mill, President C.C. MacGill and several officers of the company had gone to the offices at the end of Smith's Wharf. Before they knew it they were cut off by the flames. They were ready to jump into the harbor when Captain Vivian Phillips, of the tug "Oriole", hearing their cries through the smoke, put in and rescued them. Both sides of Pratt Street were now burning furi-

10 a.m., Monday-Bowley's Wharf to right and eastward; Gambrell's and State Tobacco Warehouses located in Pier 4, burning to right; tugs may be "Mary" and "Oriole".

ously. Sheets of flame were jumping out of warehouse windows on the west side of Commerce Street.

Earlier, the United States Revenue Cutter 'Windom", enroute to Annapolis under the command of Captain George E. McConnell, had been advised of the situation and ordered to return to Baltimore. On arrival, it was assigned to fight the fires raging through the Pratt Street piers.

Still roaring eastward through the piers,

the flames seized on the State Tobacco Warehouses Numbers 1 and 2 on the end of O'Donnell's and Dugan's Wharf, south of Wood Street between Frederick Street Dock and Long Dock. The remaining buildings of the Street Railway Power Station, just above, went unscathed. Long Dock for years before and after the fire was the point where sailing craft brought watermelons and produce from farms along the bay and oysters dredged from its depths to sell along Dugan's Wharf. Crossing Long Dock, the flames next fired the buildings along McElderry's Wharf. At the Merchants and Miners Transportation Company pier, at the foot of Mill Street below Chestnut, the steamers "Chatham" and "Kershaw" had been moved to safety earlier.

Now with the fire pressing close, the Cutter "Windom" moved into the B&O Freight Station at Locust and Hugh Streets. With the aid of B&O employees, bags of coffee were removed from the Levering Coffee Company at Mill and Locust and stowed on the decks of the "Windom" and the "Potomac" and moved to safety. Shortly thereafter the large four-story warehouse was engulfed in flames and destroyed in twenty minutes.

At 10:00 a.m. Monday, the fire at the John E. Hurst Building was raging as furiously as it had an hour after it started. By then too, the piers from Bowley's Wharf to Long Dock were ablaze and the fire had reached the west bank of the Falls.

President Ladomus of the Hanley Fire Company continues, *"They stationed our steamer at the foot of Stiles Street, where we had to carry our hose across the Falls on the top of the gas pipes spanning that stream, an undertaking few would care to do not having much of a foothold on top of pipes forty feet above the water and the wind blowing a gale,*

besides drawing 500 feet of hose. We helped save the lumberyards in that vicinity. The fire reached the Falls above and below us, but did not get within a block of where we were stationed."

The three-story Union Hospital on Union Dock between Chestnut and Locust Street, known during the Civil War as the West Hospital, burned, as well as the cotton warehouses. Packing houses and lumber yards were also ablaze. The Fireboat "Cataract" managed to beat back the flames along some sections of the dock.

Fire headquarters in New York received the urgent message that the City of Baltimore was

Levering Coffee Company, Commerce Street; firemen fighting fire during 2nd day; blanketed fire horses in foreground.

burning. Ten engines were immediately dispatched to Manhattan's Liberty Dock. Arriving, they found the ferry boat "City of Baltimore" safe at its moorings. An hour later the situation was clarified and the engines were sent to Baltimore City by train. Engine Companies 5, 26, 33, and Truck Company No. 5 arrived from New York City at 11:10 a.m. on the Pennsylvania Railroad and were rushed into the battle east of the Falls. The roof of Otto Duker's Box Factory, at President Street and Canton Avenue, caught fire but was extinguished.

Between 11:00 a.m. and 1:00 p.m., sparks and brands carried across the Falls and started large fires there. A pile of lumber adjoining warehouse No. 3 of the Broadbent and Davis Mantle Company, Canton and President Street ignited. An engine company was ordered from the Canton Avenue bridge to fight it. After a battle lasting several hours, it was extinguished.

Friendship No. 1 and Fame Hose No. 2 from Wilmington, DE, arrived at 11:30 a.m. and took draft from the harbor. The Fireboat "Cataract", commanded by Captain A. W. German, Sr., was hard at work at the foot of West Falls Avenue. A warehouse south of the icehouse on Union Dock collapsed, releasing 1,000 or more barrels of turpentine and resin. The barrel staves gave way and spurted oil over the low adjoining buildings and spilled out over the water. Blazing oil and dense smoke

obscured the sun. Both engines and the fireboat attacked the burning mass but were slowly forced back by the flames.

Monday, at 1:30 p.m., Chief Horton resumed command. Engines 7, 12, 13, 16, 27, 33 of the New York Fire Department arrived at this time, having been delayed enroute by hot boxes and derailments.

Now the flames were roaring through the lumber piles on Union Dock and threatening lumber yards and wood-working businesses on the east side. Just beyond lay a residential district peopled mainly by Jewish and Italian families. South, to City Dock, were more lumber yards, mills, and the rail yards of the President Street Station. Across from City Dock the isolated tip of Fells Point, along Dock, Block and Thames Streets extended into the outer basin to West Falls Avenue.

Dock Area - after the Fire

49

THE LAST STAND

From Baltimore Street to the Block Street drawbridge, which connected Fells Point to West Falls Avenue, five bridges crossed the Falls. Here was the last natural barrier. Here the last stand was made. Engines were placed upon the bridges and in the streets farther back for a total of thirty-seven companies. Hose lines were carried across the Falls in rowboats to combat the flames. Groups of firemen lay on the bridges, manning their hoses in the face of billowing flames, showers of red hot sparks, embers and choking smoke. At their limit of endurance, other firemen would rush in and take their places. Gradually, the flames on the west side began to subside under this constant deluge. By 3:00 o'clock, the tide of the fire began to turn.

Between 1:00 and 2:00 p.m. Monday the flames jumped to Fells Point on the east side of the Falls. The fertilizer plant of Isaac Robinson and Company at Philpot and Thames Streets exploded in flames. The flames spread to the Maine Lake Ice Company, the Sonneborn and Son Chemical Company and into the wharves along Thames Street. Directly in the line of the fire as it moved down Philpot Street was the Shryock Lumber Yard on Philpot near Thames. Its lumber shed housed over 5,000,000 ft. of lumber. Five engines, Baltimore Engines 11, 15, 18 and two from Washington were dispatched from President Street across the Block Street drawbridge.

Lombard Street Bridge; last stand made here

The cutter "Windom", too, was ordered to the yard to fight the fire from the water side. Every available hose line was brought into play. Due to the firemen's efforts, combined with a wind shift to the north, Fells Point was saved.

The Denmead Malt House, across from the City Morgue at the foot of President Street caught fire twice, and twice the firemen put out the fire before it could spread to the east.

Chief Horton had placed nine engines from New York and firemen from Atlantic City on the Merchants and Miners Savannah Wharf

Merchants & Miners Wharf Office Entrance

along Block Street at the foot of West Falls Avenue. Lumber yards on the pier blazed up repeatedly during the afternoon. One time, a steam launch with a large wooden bucket rigged upon it, put out the flames by dumping water on them. An engine from New York and Baltimore Engine 11 took suction from the Falls. Merchants and Miners tugs "Venus" and "Mary" took their hose lines as near as they dared to the dock while the engines pumped from the Falls. The "Cataract" came along, and the combined force of their streams, along with the switch of the wind to the north, pushed the fire back to the burned out area.

The storage house of the American Ice Company then blazed up. Stored within were thousands of tons of Kennebec ice, packed in sawdust. As the flames consumed the wooden structure, a glistening mountain of ice was exposed. To the south of the icehouse, the ice company's coal yards burned more slowly. This enabled the firemen to save an oyster packing plant and a saloon at the end of the pier. By their efforts, after facing an inferno for hours, not only the Savannah Wharf was saved, but the fire was stayed.

By evening, the flames, deprived of new fuel, began to subside. Fires still burned in the ruins and the lumber piles, but the worst was over.

Although the conflagration was over, the fire was far from out. Fires in the ruins continued to burn for days, and rekindled for weeks. As much as a year later, when excavating in the area for new construction, fire could still be found.

Remarkably, there was no direct loss of life due to the fire. Dr. Edwin Geer reported that 247 firemen were injured or became ill at the fire. Of these, twenty-nine were injured and the balance became ill.

As a result of exposure at the fire, three became ill and died shortly thereafter. They were Engineer Mark Kelley - Engine No. 16 - New York; Hoseman James M. McGlennen - Engine No. 7 - Baltimore City F. D.; and Lieutenant John A. McKew - Engine No. 14 - Baltimore City F. D. (severe cold developed into Tuberculosis).

American Ice Company, Federal Hill; looking towards devastation

CELEBRATION

Baltimore Jubilee Parade took place September 12, 1906

Two years after the fire, all out-of-town companies that had participated were invited back for a gigantic celebration during the Baltimore Jubilee. Nearly all responded, sending men and equipment. George Potter of Altoona, PA was among them. *"What a time we had: The railroad bought us new uniforms. The city put us up in the old Calvert Hotel free of charge. We paraded past City Hall, and were saluted by the Mayor J. Barry Mahool and the City Council. We were heroes all over again.* (George Potter was incorrect in stating that J. Barry Mahool was Mayor. At the time of the Jubilee in 1906, E. Clay Timanus served as Mayor, taking over the City after the death of Mayor McLane in 1904. Edit.)

There were free drinks, free meals. There were dances, banquets, trips to all the Baltimore firehouses, tours of the fire area, which was all but completely rebuilt. People shook our hands and thanked us for fighting the fire. It was pretty wonderful."

On September 12, 1906, a great parade of over 1400 men was held. Due to the heat of the day numerous stops were made to let the horses drink and occasionally douse their heads with water. As a result of the heat and excitement one fireman was overcome and two horses were lost. That evening a big celebration for the firemen was held at Electric Park.

Mayor E. Clay Timanus took over the operation of the city after Mayor McLane's death. He served as Mayor from 1904-1907.

Close-up of Engine # 15 Ruins. Steamer placed on wheel's so it could be drawn in parade.

Electric Park, built in 1896, this incandescent amusement park on West Belvedere Avenue and Reisterstown Road contained a race track, dance pavilion, clubhouse and casino. Here it is decorated for the Jubilee Celebration in 1906.

Sparrows Point Volunteer Fire Department Band. Sparrows Point provided manpower during the Fire, and would have marched in the Jubilee Parade.

G.W. (1983)

George Welden ended his manuscript after the description of the Jubilee of 1906. Although he did not write a closing paragraph, the editor has taken the liberty of ending the story for him.

In only two years, the City had rebuilt itself-almost 800 buildings had replaced the 1400 structures burned out by the Fire. Business was thriving, and although construction was not yet complete, many called the reconstruction amazing.

To remember the Baltimore Fire, a bronze plaque was dedicated in 1907 that stated in part:

Beginning at Liberty and German Streets the fire swept north to Fayette Street east to Jones Falls south to the Harbor. It was one of the most destructive conflagrations in the worlds history.

M.M.H. (2004)

Bronze Plaque, dedicated 1907. Located at the Fish Market between Market Place and the Jones Falls.

EPILOGUE

On February 7th, 2004, the 100th Anniversary of the Great Baltimore Fire was reached. There has been limited information recorded in two books, which have devoted all, or a large portion to the fire. The first book is the *World's Greatest Calamities - The Baltimore Fire and Chicago Horror* written by H.D. Northrop and published by The Minter Company, Harrisburg, Pa. in 1904. The second book is the *Baltimore Afire* written by Harold A. Williams and published by Schneidereith & Sons, Baltimore, Md. originally in 1954. These two volumes are the major written historical records published directly related to the fire to my knowledge and have served as background information for many articles associated with the fire.

Available to the researcher are however many newspaper accounts and stories along with periodicals, magazine articles, etc. that have been published over the last 100 years. The researcher today will find much of the information available is merely stating the same information over again. A much more in depth look at the fire is required to produce enlightening material.

This book has reached beyond the basic information to allow for a descriptive representation of what occurred on that fateful date in February, 1904.

Since George R. Welden penned this book in 1983, interest generated by the 100th anniversary is producing more research on the fire. There are several books being undertaken including a book I have written as a technical book concerning the fire department operations of both local and mutual aid responding fire departments. I am sure that researchers will continue to strive to bring forth untold tales and related information as it is discovered so that future generations may better understand what events surrounded the Baltimore Fire and its resultant effect on the City of Baltimore.

Gary E. Frederick
President
Fire Museum of Maryland

STATISTICS

Apparatus, Hose & Manpower - Baltimore City Fire Department:
(all apparatus hand or horse drawn)

Steamers	25
Combination, Chemical and Hose Wagons	26
Chemical Engines	3
Combination Hoses, Chemical & Ladder Trucks	3
Aerial Trucks	8
Water Towers	2
Fire Boat	1
Hose Carriages	7
Cotton Rubber-Lined Hose	75,000 ft.
Rubber Chemical Hose	6,500 ft.
Paid Men	463

An engine company was comprised of a steamer and a hose wagon. The steamer was a coal-fired pumping engine with a crew of two, a hostler (driver) and the engineman (engineer). The hose wagon carried the hose, the men and the fire-fighting equipment. Most hose wagons also carried two chemical tanks and a rubber chemical hose. These were known as combination wagons.

Other Cities and Towns Represented:

Alexandria, VA	unknown
Altoona, PA	1 engine
Annapolis, MD	1 engine, 2 trucks
Atlantic City, NJ	men
Baltimore County Communities:	
Hamilton	unknown
Highlandtown	1 engine
Relay, MD	1 hose reel
Roland Park	1 engine
Sparrows Point, MD	men
St. Denis, MD	2 hose reels
Westport	unknown
Chester, PA	2 engines
Hanover, PA	unknown
Harrisburg, PA	1 engine
Havre de Grace, MD	unknown
New York City, NY	5 engines, 1 truck

Philadelphia, PA	7 engines
Phoenixville, PA	men
Washington, DC	5 engines
Westminster, MD	2 hose reels, 40 men
Wilmington, DE	4 engines
Trenton, NJ	unknown
York, PA	2 engines

Specific Information from Newspaper Accounts:

Engines at fire	57
Hook and ladder trucks	11
Number of firemen	1,231
Water thrown (gallons per minute)	50,000
Number of hose streams	100
Fires from sparks	52
Number of buildings destroyed	1,526
Acres of ground fire-swept	140
Hose burned (feet)	29,900
Loss (estimated by Insurance Committee)	$50 million
Insured for	$32 million
Insurance paid	$29 million
Lives lost	0
Slightly hurt	150
Persons injured	60
Died of exposure	3

Fire Plugs used by Baltimore Engines:

Engine Co.	Number of Plugs	Engine Co.	Number of Plugs
1	5	6	4
2	5	7	6
3	3	8	1*
4	5	9	2
5	6	10	4

Engine Co.	Number of Plugs	Engine Co.	Number of Plugs
11	2	18	5
12	3	19	2
13	2	20	4
14	3	21	9
15-1	(destroyed)	22	7
15-2	4	23	7
16	7	24	(not in service)
17	2	25	7

*47 hrs. on Baltimore St., west of Liberty Street

	Sequence of Alarms – Sunday Feb. 7, 1904	
Time	*Box*	*Location*
10:44 AM	266	McElderry & Eden
10:48 AM	854	Hurst & Co. (automatic)
10:51 AM	447	Baltimore & Liberty
10:55 AM	414	German & Howard (general alarm)
11:05 AM	513	Lombard & Sharp
11:13 AM	41	Fayette & St. Paul
11:41 AM	218	Low & Front
11:47 AM	204	Monument & Caroline
11:48 AM	219	Holliday & Fayette
12:00 NOON	266	McElderry & Eden
12:16 PM	211	Front & Hillen
12:41 PM	226	Orleans & Forrest
1:16 PM	32	St. Paul & Saratoga
1:54 PM	422	Fayette & Howard
2:20 PM	31	Calvert & Pleasant
2:43 PM	248	Bath & Holliday
4:00 PM	31	Calvert & Pleasant
6:52 PM	318	Charles & Barnet
7:50 PM	224	Preston & Druid Hill
8:00 PM	21	Gay & Saratoga
9:00 PM	214	Exeter & Fayette

Street widths of some of the critical streets in the fire area are listed below to better illustrate the problems involved.

Widths given are from curb to curb. Telegraph poles and other obstructions confined wheeled traffic to these limits.

German - Street - west of Hopkins Place	40 feet
German - Street - east of Hopkins Place	20 feet
Hanover Street	40 feet
Liberty Street	40 feet
Baltimore Street	40 feet
Pratt Street	40 feet
Fayette Street	40 feet
Hopkins Place	30 feet
Charles Street	30 feet
Lexington Street	30 feet
Lombard Street - west of Charles	40 feet
Lombard Street - east of Charles	30 feet
St. Paul Street - Lexington to Fayette	20 feet
St. Paul Street - Fayette to Baltimore	15 feet
Light Street - Baltimore to Pratt.	25 feet
Light Street - Pratt Street south	40 feet
Little Sharp Street	10 feet
McClellan's Alley	10 feet

Pavements (sidewalks) for these streets ranged in width from approximately 15 ft. for the wider streets, to 5 ft. or less for the narrow ones. Generally speaking, the distance between buildings on opposite sides of the street would be the street width plus the sidewalks, i.e. the total building to building width for Hanover Street was approximately 70 feet, while that of McClellan's Alley was as little as 20 feet.

G.W. (1983)

George Welden completed his research in 1983. Since then, further information has been found that updates these figures. See Gary Frederick's publication, *Fire Department Operations: A Technical Report/The Great Baltimore Fire*, 2004, for further details.

M.M.H. (2004)

BIBLIOGRAPHY & RESOURCES

BOOKS

Cassedy, J. Albert. *The Firemen's Record.* Baltimore, MD: Firemen's Relief Fund, 1911.

Glory, C.O. *100 Years of Glory: 1871-1971 – District of Columbia Fire Department.*
    Washington, DC: Mount Vernon Publishing Co., 1971.

Jones, Arthur B. *The Salem Fire.* Boston, MA: Gotham Press, 1914.

Morris, John V. *Fires and Firefighters.* Boston, MA: Little, Brown & Company, 1953.

Murray, William A. *The Unheralded Heroes.* Baltimore, MD: E. John Schmitz & Sons, 1969.

National Fire Protection Association. *The Baltimore Conflagration.* Boston, MA: NFPA, 1904.

Northrop, H.D. *World's Greatest Calamities.* Washington, DC: Northrop, 1904.

Rukert, Norman G. *The Fells Point Story.* Baltimore, MD: Bodine & Assoc., Inc., 1976.

Williams, Harold A. *Baltimore Afire.* Baltimore, MD: Schneidereith & Sons, 1954.

MAGAZINES

Firehouse Magazine
The Baltimore Scene - Jan., Feb., 1964
Folks News & Views - Vol. X - Baltimore Gas & Electric Co.
American History Illustrated - The National Historical Society
Fire Engineering - Sept., 1973

NEWSPAPERS

Baltimore Sun
Baltimore Sunday Sun
Baltimore Sun Magazine

BROCHURES

Story of the Fire - Christhilf, Litsinger, Christhilf
Official Book of the Baltimore Fire
The Book of The Fire - D. M. Henderson
The Modern Fire Protection - Baltimore National Automatic Fire Alarm Co.

G.W. (1983)

PHOTO CREDITS

B&O Railroad Museum: 21-top

Nancy Bramucci: 33

Fire Museum of Maryland: 8, 10-middle, 10-bottom, 11-bottom, 12, 14-left, 14-right, 15-top, 16-bottom, 17-top right, 17-lower left, 17-lower right, 18-upper left, 19, 20-top, 20-bottom, 21-bottom, 23-top, 26, 29-bottom, 31, 32, 34, 35, 36, 37-top, 38, 39-right, 40-middle, 42-bottom, 44, 45, 49, 50-bottom, 52, 53

Gary Frederick: 48

Stephen G. Heaver, Jr.: 9 (Map Annotations)

Maryland Division, Enoch Pratt Free Library: 10-top, 13, 16-top, 18-lower left, 18-lower right, 20-middle, 23-bottom, 25, 27, 29-top, 30, 37-middle, 39-left, 39-bottom, 40-top, 40-right, 41-top, 41-bottom, 42-top, 43, 46, 47, 50-top, 51

Maryland State Archives: 37

National Automatic Fire Alarm Co.: 11-right

Peale Collection (now part of Maryland Historical Society): 15-bottom

Wayne Schaumberg: 11-left

Sun Papers Archive: 22

Pauline Welden: 7, 9

INDEX